The *Learning Communities Guide* to
IMPROVING READING INSTRUCTION

This book is dedicated to our husbands, Arlen Gregory and Peter Nikas, who have supported our passion for reading, writing, and leading. This book also is dedicated to the thousands of leaders and teachers who are committed to creating professional learning communities where teaching and learning for literacy thrive.

The *Learning Communities Guide* to
IMPROVING READING INSTRUCTION

Valerie Hastings Gregory — **Jan Rozzelle Nikas**
Foreword by Richard DuFour and Rebecca DuFour

CORWIN PRESS
A Sage Publications Company
Thousand Oaks, California

For information:

 Corwin Press
A Sage Publications Company
2455 Teller Road
Thousand Oaks, California 91320
www.corwinpress.com

Sage Publications Ltd.
1 Oliver's Yard
55 City Road
London, EC1Y 1SP
United Kingdom

Sage Publications India Pvt. Ltd.
B-42, Panchsheel Enclave
Post Box 4109
New Delhi 110 017 India

Printed in the United States of America

Library of Congress Cataloging-in-Publication Data

Gregory, Valerie Hastings.
The learning communities guide to improving reading instruction / by Valerie Hastings Gregory and M. Jan Rozzelle.
    p. cm.
Includes bibliographical references and index.
ISBN 0-7619-3175-9 (cloth) — ISBN 0-7619-3176-7 (pbk.)
    1. Reading—United States. 2. Teacher participation in administration—United States. 3. Educational accountability—United States. I. Rozzelle, M. Jan. II. Title.
LB1050.2.G74 2005
372.41—dc22

                                        2004009117

"Mind" from *Things of this World*, copyright (c) 1956 and renewed 1984 by Richard Wilbur. Reprinted by permission of Harcourt, Inc.

This book is printed on acid-free paper.

05   06   07   08   09   10   9   8   7   6   5   4   3   2   1

Acquisitions Editor:	Jean Ward
Production Editor:	Kristen Gibson
Copy Editor:	Ruth Saavedra
Typesetter:	C & M Digitals (P) Ltd.
Proofreader:	Penclope Sippel
Indexer:	David Luljak
Cover Designer:	Michael Dubowe

CONTENTS

FOREWORD

With the enactment of the educational reform legislation titled No Child Left Behind (NCLB), the United States has, in effect, boldly proclaimed that all children will learn—or else. The motivation behind NCLB legislation has been widely debated. Proponents portray the initiative as a sincere attempt to guarantee that every child, particularly poor and minority students, receive an education that leads to high levels of learning. Opponents contend the legislation is unrealistic and simplistic at best or a thinly veiled attempt to dismantle the public system of education at worst. Regardless of the motivation, contemporary public schools in the United States are being called upon to achieve a standard that goes far beyond the goals of any previous generation—high levels of learning for all students. Furthermore, NCLB threatens schools and the educators within them with escalating sanctions if they fail to meet newly imposed standards. The rationale behind this approach suggests that educators have always known how to help all kids learn but have been too disinterested in the welfare of their students or too lazy to put forth the necessary effort. Fear is needed to provide the necessary motivation—either perform or risk closing your school and/or losing your job.

In *The Learning Communities Guide to Improving Reading Instruction,* Valerie Gregory and Jan Rozzelle Nikas embrace the premise that schools and the educators within them must be committed to the learning of each child entrusted to them. They make a compelling argument that helping each student develop the ability to read with high levels of comprehension is an absolute prerequisite if the concept of "learning for all" is to move from politically correct hyperbole to reality in our nation's schools. They make it clear, however, that they honor teachers and teaching, that they believe educators have the best interests of their students at heart, and most importantly, that training and support are more effective than threats in helping teachers meet the formidable challenges they face in their classrooms. Their book is based on the premise that educators have both the willingness and ability to become more effective if the culture of their schools focuses on the ongoing learning, continuous improvement, and professional growth of the adults. They set out to provide solid information, specific strategies, and much-needed encouragement to teachers—and they succeed at every level.

There is much to commend in this book. One of its greatest strengths is the way in which the authors provide specific, pragmatic, proven strategies to teach literacy in ways that teachers can apply immediately in their classrooms. Too often researchers and practitioners hold different interests, speak

viii THE LEARNING
COMMUNITIES
GUIDE TO
IMPROVING
READING
INSTRUCTION

different languages, and live in different worlds. Too often they hold each other in low regard. This book does a wonderful job of bridging the chasm that often exists between the separate worlds of higher education and K–12 educators. It applies powerful research findings and nontechnical, jargon-free advice for classroom teachers. The authors demonstrate an understanding of and appreciation for the K–12 setting that can come only with working extensively in that environment.

For example, the Reading Reflection Survey presented in Chapter 7 represents a powerful instrument for the improvement of a literacy program that a school could use in a number of different ways. An individual teacher could use the guide to reflect upon and assess his or her instruction. A team of teachers could use it to gather data on the practices at their grade level and to develop an action plan for improvement. An entire school could use it as a basis for identifying areas that require focused training. The guide—like the book in general—is powerful, pragmatic, and beneficial to real teachers and schools.

A second strength of *The Learning Communities Guide to Improving Reading Instruction* is the authors' recognition of the link between adult learning and student learning. Throughout the book Gregory and Rozzelle Nikas call for increased attention to and support of powerful professional development as a linchpin of any effort to help all students achieve at high levels. Moreover, they make it clear that the professional development they envision is more likely to occur in the workplace than the workshop. Again, their respect for educators is evident as they describe schools in which teachers work together to identify areas of concern and build the shared knowledge necessary to address those concerns. The focused, sustained, teacher-led professional development they describe is essential to the success of any school committed to learning for all of its students.

Finally, *The Learning Communities Guide to Improving Reading Instruction* does not simply present a new program for teaching literacy: It calls for the creation of a unique school culture. In the school the authors describe, educators share a strong sense of purpose: high levels of learning for all students. In order to achieve that purpose, they work together collaboratively, engage in collective inquiry, participate in action research, embed continuous improvement processes into their routine practices, and monitor their effectiveness on the basis of tangible results. In other words, the educators in the school move beyond merely implementing programs and instead focus upon building their collective capacity to function as a professional learning community.

The reference to "professional learning communities" in the title of this book carries profound implications, as each word presents a challenge to educators. A professional is someone with expertise in a specialized field, an individual who has not only pursued advanced training to enter the field but who is also expected to remain current in its evolving knowledge base. In the scenarios presented by Gregory and Rozzelle Nikas teachers do more than pool opinions. They investigate emerging research and build shared knowledge of best practice in order to better achieve their common goals. In short, they act professionally.

Learning suggests ongoing action and perpetual curiosity. In Chinese, the term *learning* is represented by two characters: The first means "to study" and the second means "to practice constantly." In the situations presented in this book, educators engage in the ongoing study and constant practice that characterize a commitment to their own learning. Furthermore, an emphasis on learning shifts the focus of a staff from inputs to outcomes, from intentions to results. When educators regard teaching as the primary purpose of their school, they are driven by questions such as "Did every student have access to the appropriate curriculum?" and "Are the instructional materials and strategies appropriate?" Their focus is on whether or not students have been taught. When educators regard learning as the fundamental purpose of their school, the most pressing questions become, "Is each student mastering the intended outcomes?" and "What can we do to assist students who experience initial difficulty?" The difference between a focus on teaching and a focus on learning is much more than semantics, and so the term *learning* community carries significant implications.

Finally, while much has been written about learning organizations, Gregory and Rozzelle Nikas chose to use the term *community*. In an organization, the emphasis is on structure and efficiency. *Community*, on the other hand, suggests a group linked by common interests and a place of emotional support. When teachers create an environment in which people work together and support one another to accomplish collectively what they could not possibly accomplish by working in isolation, they are clearly building community.

This book will be an invaluable resource for any school practitioner—teacher, principal, literacy coach, or instructional coordinator—who recognizes that literacy is the door of opportunity through which a student must enter to truly learn at high levels and avoid being left behind. We highly recommend it to all educators who hope to open that door for every child entrusted to them.

—*Richard DuFour*
—*Rebecca DuFour*

PREFACE

Our work with schools has reinforced our deep belief that professional learning communities are our best hope for sustaining improved teaching and learning in literacy. Through years of classroom observations and school-based professional development, we have collaborated with leadership teams to create and refine a network of learning experiences to support teachers. This book reflects what we learned from working with leaders and teachers with limited knowledge, experiences, and instructional repertoires for improving reading. Therefore, this book is a professional development resource that includes basic knowledge and instructional tools to improve teaching and learning in reading. We hope leaders, literacy coaches, and leadership teams find this resource to be as useful to them as they have been to us in working with partner schools of the College of William and Mary.

ACKNOWLEDGMENTS

We acknowledge and thank the following individuals who supported or contributed to the creation of this book: Pat Bishop, Ann Conzemius, Kathy Farwell, Carolyn Felling, Barbara Goldstein, Lisa Hill, Toni Hollingsworth, Denise Johnson, Judy Johnston, Craig Kauffman, Michele Mitchell-Moffit, Jan O'Neill, Rosemary Rice-Jones, Gay Robinson, Carol Scearce, and Ed Wallent. In particular, we are grateful for the work of P. David Pearson, Michael Pressley, and Barbara Taylor, whose work with the Center for the Improvement of Early Reading Achievement (CIERA) inspired our own work.

We especially thank the following colleagues for reading, reviewing, and advising us on this manuscript: Richard DuFour, Rebecca DuFour, Robin Fogarty, Carole Geiger, Gay Ivey, and our editor, Jean Ward.

Last, much of this work was made possible through funding from the Jessie Ball duPont Fund, which supported the Partnership for Improving Leading and Learning in Rural Schools Project (PILLRS). We were also fortunate to be informed by the work and research of the Center for Gifted Education at the College of William and Mary, led by Dr. Joyce Van Tassel-Baska, and to have the constant support of Virginia McLaughlin, Chancellor Professor and Dean of the School of Education at the College of William and Mary.

ABOUT THE AUTHORS

Valerie Hastings Gregory has devoted much of her professional life to shaping professional learning communities in schools. She has promoted effective professional development as a school building, central office, and Virginia Department of Education administrator for elementary education and gifted education. Valerie is an educational consultant for assessment, curriculum, instruction, and leadership at Fogarty and Associates, Pearson Professional Development, QLD Learning, and the School Leadership Institute for the College of William and Mary. Valerie received her doctorate in Educational Policy Planning and Leadership from the College of William and Mary, where she extensively studied conditions for transfer of professional development to classroom practice. While a doctoral student, Valerie received the Outstanding Doctoral Student Award from the National Association for Education of the Gifted. In addition to this book, Valerie is the author of two other books, *Conditions That Support Transfer for Change* and *Problem-Based Learning in Social Studies.*

In her position as Director of the William and Mary School Leadership Institute, **Jan Rozzelle Nikas** directs multiple school reform partnerships with Virginia public school districts. One partnership with five rural school districts has focused on improving leading and learning in 15 schools for the past 4 years, particularly in the area of literacy. Prior to her position at the university, Jan served a large suburban school district as reading coordinator of professional development, curriculum, and instruction for 52 schools. Her research interests focus on what works in improving literacy teaching and learning, and leadership development of principals and teachers. Jan is a past president of the Virginia State Reading Association (VSRA) and recipient of the Reading Teacher of the Year Award from VSRA. Jan also received the Collaborative Leadership Award and was awarded the Frances B. & Robert O. Nelson Memorial Scholarship for Character, Commitment, and Achievement.

Considering How to Lead Schoolwide Improvement in Reading

1

Imagine this . . .

You walk into the school conference room early in August. You see that the superintendent is already there to meet with the school leadership team about recently released test scores. Your school did not make adequate yearly progress in reading. You already met the principal, also new to the school, but this is the first time you meet the grade-level chairs, the reading teacher, and the assistant principal. After introductions, the superintendent gets right down to business by stating, "The reading test results need to improve. I want you to know that reading is a priority in our district and I believe success in reading is key to achievement in all content areas through high school. What can I do to support your efforts?" The principal looks everyone in the eye and says, "What are your thoughts, team? What will WE do to improve OUR students' reading performance?"

This scenario reflects the plight of many schools we work with and illustrates what school leadership teams encounter in an age of heightened accountability. More than ever before, we need a clear vision about quality reading instruction. Also, the stakes are high for schools to take steps necessary to attain that vision. But there is good news. Research enlightens us about what works and what does not work in the integrated arenas of reading instruction, school leadership, and professional development. Educators are challenged to

2 THE LEARNING
COMMUNITIES
GUIDE TO
IMPROVING
READING
INSTRUCTION

become familiar with what is known about quality teaching, leadership, and professional development and to transfer that knowledge to practice in an ongoing, consistent, systematic way.

We believe that effective leadership is essential to improve the teaching and learning of reading. Furthermore, we think that leadership in professional learning communities includes all teachers and administrators who have the desire and the initiative to make a difference in student reading performance. This book provides leaders focused on quality reading instruction with knowledge and tools for school improvement that leave no child or teacher behind.

Effective school leadership teams create learning communities where continuous learning is not limited to students between the ages of five and eighteen. The adults in the building are learners as well and model lifelong learning through ongoing reflection on teaching and learning. Stories of successful schools reveal that deep and abiding change is a difficult task that requires the cohesive efforts of school teams. Effective leaders build cohesion by shaping cultures that honor and support continuous learning and recognize the collegial and social aspects of learning. Thus, effective leaders initiate professional learning communities to encourage, not discourage, continued growth in practice. These leaders accomplish this task using a variety of professional development experiences that target student achievement.

Building professional learning communities will not necessarily lead to improvement in teaching and learning unless such communities engage in focused, sustained, content-driven professional growth experiences. In other words, effective leaders identify focused efforts that address the right content, in the right way, at the right time, in a culture that is conducive to continuous learning. Quality professional development integrates pedagogy with the content that teachers deliver, in the schools where they teach.

Based on our experience, we suggest that school leaders intent on improving teaching and learning in reading consider a framework of six broad elements: (1) personalizing reading instruction, (2) managing environments for literacy, (3) ensuring student engagement, (4) emphasizing active teaching, (5) targeting comprehension, and (6) creating professional learning communities (Figure 1.1).

Subsequent chapters describe each of these elements. The organization of each chapter includes a scenario, the research base, sample strategies, a summary of the big ideas presented in the chapter, and a constructive reflection. The constructive reflections are designed as tools for school-based professional development that fosters supportive learning communities.

Chapter 2 targets the primary focus of any literacy improvement effort: student needs. This chapter addresses the question, *How can teachers personalize reading instruction?* Shaping effective literacy instruction begins with matching books to students, and this requires teachers to get to know them. The extent to which teachers know their students determines the effectiveness of their reading instruction. In getting to know students, we must consider a variety of factors before a clear picture emerges. Strategies for getting to know students include those that reveal student interests, strengths, needs, level of reading, strategy use, and learning preferences. Chapter 2 addresses routines and strategies for getting to know students and personalizing reading instruction.

⊙ Figure 1.1   Framework for Improving Reading Instruction

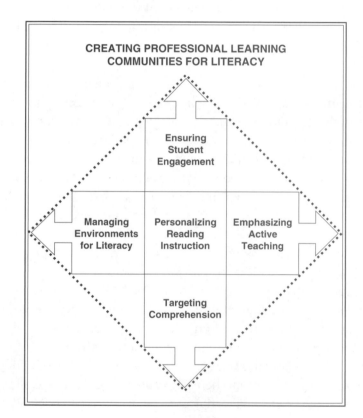

Managing Environments for Literacy

➢ Positive, productive environment?
➢ Types of texts?
➢ Grouping?
➢ Schedules & space?
➢ Routines & centers

Personalizing Reading Instruction

➢ Differentiating instruction?
➢ Getting to know students?
➢ Matching students to texts?
➢ Using assessments to personalize?
➢ Sample differentiated lessons?

Planning Active Teaching

➢ Exemplary teaching?
➢ Teaching & learning zone?
➢ Student-supported teaching?
➢ Organizing instruction?
➢ Planning instruction?

CREATING PROFESSIONAL LEARNING COMMUNITIES FOR LITERACY

Ensuring Student Engagement

Managing Environments for Literacy

Personalizing Reading Instruction

Emphasizing Active Teaching

Targeting Comprehension

Ensuring Student Engagement

➢ Time, text, talk, & tasks?
➢ Metacognition & reading?
➢ Promoting self-regulated readers?
➢ Intervention tools?
➢ Promoting higher level thinking and talk about text?

Creating Professional Learning Communities for Literacy

➢ "Look fors" for literacy?
➢ Reading observation & reflection survey?
➢ Using data to set goals?
➢ Leadership for change?
➢ School-based professional development?

Targeting Comprehension

➢ Seven comprehension strategies?
➢ Sample mini lessons?
➢ Vocabulary building?
➢ Comprehension & vocabulary tools?

4

THE LEARNING
COMMUNITIES
GUIDE TO
IMPROVING
READING
INSTRUCTION

Managing environments for literacy is the second element for shaping quality reading instruction. What are effective strategies and practices for managing literacy environments? Effective classroom management either promotes or thwarts quality reading instruction. We find that teachers frequently have concerns about issues of classroom management. How should I group my students? What do I need to do to help students work cooperatively and productively? What are other students doing while I am with a guided reading group? What materials are essential to effective teaching and learning? What routines are necessary to provide an environment that is conducive to student learning? These questions and others are answered in Chapter 3.

The third element for improving literacy instruction is *ensuring student engagement.* How do exemplary teachers increase student engagement? Linked to active teaching, active student engagement in reading, writing, and talking about text influences whether high gains in reading are achieved. Chapter 4 describes specific research-based strategies that promote active student engagement rather than passive responses to reading.

Chapter 5, emphasizes active teaching, the fourth element of effective literacy programs. What is active teaching and what do exemplary teachers do to facilitate active learning? Research indicates that active teaching strategies positively influence student achievement in reading. What research-based active teaching strategies should teachers use to promote high achievement in reading and writing? How should the varied active learning strategies be implemented? Effective literacy programs examine the extent to which teachers engage in active teaching and provide professional development that builds requisite skills and knowledge.

Targeting comprehension is another crucial element for improving reading. The ultimate goal of all reading instruction is reading comprehension—that is, reading *is* comprehending. What must teachers do to target comprehension so that all students read at higher levels? While beginning reading instruction emphasizes phonemic awareness, phonics, fluency, vocabulary, and comprehension, researchers agree that "comprehension is the reason for reading" (Armburster, Lehr, & Osborn, 2001, p. 48). Effective reading instruction requires teachers to model specific comprehension strategies and provide adequate time for students to practice strategies that good readers use (Pressley, 2002). What strategies promote comprehension? How can educators more thoughtfully teach comprehension strategies? Chapter 6 responds to these questions.

Chapter 7 discusses the importance of *creating professional learning communities for literacy.* Effective instructional leadership is inclusive, with teachers and administrators working collaboratively to improve literacy instruction. How can professional learning communities provide leadership for literacy? What school leaders do to promote and support effective reading instruction is fundamental to positive, sustained change in classrooms. What do leaders need to know about best practices in reading instruction? How can leaders encourage implementation of these best practices? What are the conditions for change and how can these conditions be fostered in schools and classrooms? How can leaders promote professional development that targets transfer of effective content and instructional practices in reading?

A reflection tool for school leadership teams to use is introduced in Chapter 7. This tool identifies "look fors" associated with teacher engagement, student engagement, instructional content, grouping patterns, and reading materials. Chapter 7 also suggests how the reflection tool can be used to identify gaps between current practice and research-based practices for reading instruction.

Why read this book? Because you want to create professional learning communities to improve reading instruction and increase student performance in reading. We present a framework of best practices for improving reading instruction and tools for reflecting on and assessing current practice. Also, we want to make leadership teams aware of effective professional development approaches for improving literacy instruction. The elements presented in the framework are components of an observation and reflection tool used in over 300 classrooms. We based this tool on current research conducted by the Center for the Improvement of Early Reading Achievement (Taylor & Pearson, 2000). The Reading Reflection Survey presented in Chapter 7 helps school leaders identify priorities and goals for improving reading instruction. Specifically, this tool enables school leaders to assess current practice and create action plans for professional development.

CONSTRUCTIVE REFLECTIONS

After reading this chapter about the framework for improving reading instruction, describe which element you think should be targeted first in your own professional practice. Explain why you believe this element should be addressed first and share your beliefs with your teaching team.

Complete the following "thinking at right angles" graphic organizer by listing three things you learned from reading this chapter (Figure 1.2). Also list feelings you experienced from reading the chapter and describe what your next step will be. Share your thoughts with your team.

Figure 1.2   Thinking at Right Angles for Reflecting on Chapter 1

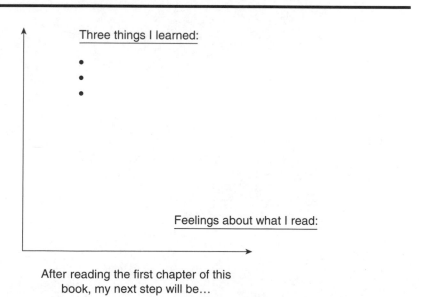

Three things I learned:

-
-
-

Feelings about what I read:

After reading the first chapter of this
book, my next step will be...

Personalizing Reading Instruction 2

I magine this . . .

The fifth-grade classroom buzzes with the conversations of students as they talk excitedly about their reading with classmates. It appears that students' enthusiasm about reading stems from their diverse interests and backgrounds being honored as they apply what they learn about comprehension to books of their choice. One group of boys has formed a reading club that devours books about the westward movement. They became interested in this topic because it was related to a fifth-grade social studies standard; however, the boys' immersion in literature about the west has carried them beyond the fifth-grade curriculum. They plan to share what they have learned about westward expansion by preparing a display for the school lobby. Another group of students has been reading a series of personal memoirs and is intrigued with the idea of creating a book of personal memoirs about their parents. Coming from diverse cultures and backgrounds, the parents offer rich stories as the students interview several in one corner of the classroom. A third group of students is interested in NASCAR and has been reading various leveled texts, including magazine articles, Internet texts, and books, about this topic. The teacher has created a classroom library that reflects the interests, strengths, and needs of her students. She was able to do this because she devoted the beginning of the school year to learning about her students and their families.

Do you really embrace the idea that all children can learn? Do you differentiate between teaching and learning so that teaching is all about what you do to make sure that all students will learn? Our students come to us with rich backgrounds and varied interests that influence their motivation to read, the topics they choose to read, and the success with which they read. If all children are to learn to read at high levels, teachers must make reading a personal experience for all learners and take every opportunity to personalize

8 THE LEARNING
COMMUNITIES
GUIDE TO
IMPROVING
READING
INSTRUCTION

instruction. This personalization begins with getting to know students' strengths, weaknesses, interests, and backgrounds and continues as the teacher weaves this information into a rich tapestry of learning experiences that focus on reading comprehension. The wise teacher knows that motivation to read grows out of students' interests and that teachers must discover those topics that interest each learner and find reading material they can read easily. This chapter describes considerations for personalizing reading instruction.

WHAT SHOULD WE CONSIDER WHEN PLANNING TO DIFFERENTIATE LITERACY INSTRUCTION?

Exemplary teachers consider how to personalize or differentiate literacy instruction to accommodate diverse student strengths and needs. This complex task overwhelms novice teachers who may need a concrete framework to consider how to differentiate instruction. Teachers can apply four types of strategies to accomplish this complex task: environmental strategies, content strategies, process strategies, and product strategies. *Environmental strategies* create a climate that celebrates diversity and nurtures a community of literacy learners. *Content strategies* enrich literacy instruction by incorporating adjustable assignments, themes, controversial issues, and curriculum compacting. *Process strategies* target how the teacher embraces students' diverse learning styles to create relevant learning experiences that improve reading and writing. *Product strategies* target how students can demonstrate acquisition of strategies and skills in diverse ways, using authentic reading and writing. Figure 2.1 provides a four-corner framework of strategies that support teacher teams' attempts to differentiate literacy instruction. Exemplary teachers adopt strategies in all four areas.

HOW CAN WE GET TO KNOW STUDENTS' INTERESTS?

Dewey advised that to be successful in educating our children we must first find out what interests them (Dewey, 1913). Think about it—are you always motivated to read or are you motivated to read certain genres or topics? For example, we love to read travel magazines and dream about those journeys we have not yet made. No one needs to encourage us to read about travel—we do it on our own and, with great enthusiasm, we discuss what we have read with each other. On the other hand, we could care less about NASCAR. We seldom choose to read about NASCAR and would only do so if there was some compelling reason. We are not interested in this topic, nor would we likely discuss it, even though we realize that it attracts more fans than any other sport. (We aren't even sure why they call it a sport.)

The same is true of our students. We might think that some of them are not motivated to read, but usually the case is that they are not motivated to read what *we* want them to read. Thus, if we want to help our students develop a passion

◉ Figure 2.1   Four-Corner Framework for Differentiating Literacy Instruction

ENVIRONMENTAL STRATEGIES

- Create a climate that celebrates diversity.
- Determine learners' interests, learning styles, and knowledge.
- Use varied grouping options to address learners' needs.
- Organize a classroom library with diverse genres, topics, and reading levels.
- Provide a rich environment with multisensory and varied materials and manipulatives.
- Provide an audience for student work and create exhibits.
- Arrange "spaces" for whole group, small group, and individual learning experiences.
- Provide opportunities for students to choose books to read and pieces to write.

CONTENT STRATEGIES

- Adapt literacy objectives to make them more simple or complex, using adjustable assignments.
- Incorporate concept-based curriculum using themes such as change, communities, patterns, systems, and so on.
- Focus on integrating content-related issues and controversies in teaching reading and writing.
- Compact the curriculum to reflect learner needs by: (1) defining the goals and outcomes of a particular unit or segment of instruction, (2) determining and documenting which students have already mastered most or all of a set of learning outcomes, and (3) providing acceleration or enrichment options for students who have demonstrated mastery.

PROCESS STRATEGIES

- Adapt the learning process to engage varied levels of thinking skills.
- Incorporate multiple intelligences and learning styles (see Figure 3.3).
- Use graphic organizers, advanced organizers, and other nonlinguistic representations to scaffold learning about reading, writing, and speaking.
- Use varied questions to guide student reflection about literature and writing.
- Utilize integrated, real-world curricular and instructional approaches.
- Consider and use gradual release of responsibility to model, scaffold, and coach (see Figure 5.3).

PRODUCT STRATEGIES

- Provide opportunities for students to share what they know about reading and writing in varied ways.
- Employ authentic assessments that use rubrics to provide specific feedback on reading, writing, and speaking.
- Utilize real-world texts as models for student products.
- Encourage students to reflect upon their work and how they learn.

for reading and an ability to read at higher levels, we must care about what they care about and bring related materials into our classrooms for them to read. Our primary goals are to instill a love of reading and the ability to apply comprehension strategies independently in a wide variety of texts. To accomplish these goals teachers may consider going outside of the "basal box." Instead, we can hook students on literature to unlock the secrets of comprehension. *Hooked on literature* means students are exposed to a wide array of interesting texts they want to read because the literature means something to them and is easy for them to read. Personalizing reading builds interest in reading, especially among our struggling readers, from backgrounds of poverty. "Central to fostering enhanced interest in voluntary reading is providing a substantial degree of autonomy in the choice of text to be read and a substantial quantity of books that vary on several dimensions, including difficulty, genre, topic, and length" (Allington & McGill-Franzen, 2003, p. 73). Choice is a key element of motivation.

Personalizing reading instruction means teachers take time to get to know their students. There are many ways teachers can accomplish this important task. They can interview students, interview students' parents, observe social interactions, use surveys, and give students writing prompts. One strategy we have used involves a combination of writing prompts and social interactions. At the beginning of the year, we ask students to respond to several prompts that address learning preferences and interests. Figure 2.2 shows this personal reflection that we use at the beginning of the year with upper-grade students. Teachers may adapt this for younger students. We like to have the students respond to chunks of the stems on a daily basis, for example #1–5 the first day, #6–10 the second day, and so on. After students have responded to the daily stem statements, we play music and ask them to carry their responses to the stem statements with them as they move to the music around the room. When the music stops, the students are asked to share one of their personal responses with the nearest student. When the music begins, students once again move around the room repeating the process with a different personal response until responses to all five stem statements have been shared. We like to observe and listen as the students interact with each other.

The next day, the process is repeated as students respond to five more stem statements and share personal responses with their peers. Finally, after three days, students have responded to and shared responses to all fifteen stem statements, the teacher has a wealth of knowledge about the students and the students have gotten to know each other better.

We also like students to write poems and class books about themselves during the first weeks of school. An effective getting-to-know-you experience is having students write an "I wish" poem (Worthy, Broaddus, & Ivey, 2001). Using the format of Kenneth Koch's "wishes poem" (Koch, 1970, pp. 64–86), each student writes one sentence that will become a part of a class poem. The steps for writing "I wish" poems follow:

- Students identify three categories (i.e., favorite celebrity, favorite pastime, favorite dessert).

- Each student writes one sentence that starts with the words "I wish."

- Sentences are compiled into one class poem that the teacher reads aloud to the class.

- The poem is read again with students reading their own sentences (Worthy et al., 2001).

Figure 2.2 Writing Prompts for Getting to Know Student Preferences and
Interests

GETTING TO KNOW YOU . . .

Using Personal Reflection

1. If I could be anything, I would be . . .

2. I spend most of my time with . . .

3. I like to learn by . . .

4. I don't like to learn by . . .

5. I feel uncomfortable when . . .

6. I feel most comfortable when . . .

7. My favorite book is . . . because . . .

8. If I could meet anyone, I would like to meet . . . because . . .

9. When I have free time, I like to . . .

10. The best thing about me is . . .

11. Something I would like others to know about me is . . .

12. I like music that . . .

13. I prefer working . . . (in a group or alone) because . . .

14. My dream is to . . .

15. Another stem statement for reflection I'd like to be given is . . .

The rewards that come from getting to know students' preferences and interests are great: increased learning, decreased behavior problems, and the development of self-directed, independent readers. Teacher teams that take the time to learn about their students find that they can hook students on reading by using their interests as bait.

WHAT IS THE LINK BETWEEN STUDENT MOTIVATION, ATTITUDE, EFFICACY, AND READING MATERIALS?

Have you ever read a text that was difficult for you to comprehend? How did you feel? What did you do? If there was no compelling reason for you to read the difficult text, you may have abandoned it and determined that it wasn't worth your effort to read because you probably wouldn't be able to understand it anyway. Think about the students in your classroom who struggle to read difficult text. Chances are, like you, they give up because they don't think they will succeed in reading and comprehending—especially if they did not choose the book.

Motivation is "an intrinsic desire to initiate, sustain, and direct one's activity" (Morrow, 1997, p. 4). Several factors impact whether students are motivated to read. We have already mentioned that it is important for teachers to consider student interests in the reading process if we want them to be motivated to read. But interest is not enough. When children are given choices in what they read, they feel a sense of control that is motivating. Then there is the issue of social collaboration—the basis for adult book clubs. We love to talk about what we read, and our motivation is increased by interacting with others about what we have read. Students are like us—they are motivated by talking with their peers about interesting text. The issue of challenge is also an important factor in student motivation to read. If something is too easy, students lose focus and interest, and if something is too challenging they feel threatened and give up. Thus, if we want students to be motivated to read, we need to adopt the Goldilocks Principle and provide students with reading material that is just right. When teachers apply the Goldilocks Principle, students are able to complete the reading task successfully; therefore, they gain a sense of accomplishment about their reading.

HOW CAN WE MATCH STUDENTS TO TEXT?

"Creating classroom environments in which successful reading is the norm—for all children—will mean creating classrooms in which children are well matched to the books they are reading" (Allington & McGill-Franzen, 2003, p. 73). When we give every child in the classroom the same book, we are not setting them up for successful reading. The one-size-fits-all mentality may result in some students either becoming bored or believing they can't be readers. This will not help eliminate the reading achievement gap. How can we provide that just-right text that each student can read accurately, fluently, and with understanding?

The Goldilocks Principle helps identify the just-right books that students need to be successful readers. Think about the story "Goldilocks and the Three Bears." Goldilocks was on a mission to find those just-right things that addressed her needs and preferences. Her chair could not be too big or small—it had to be just right. Her porridge could not be too hot or too cold—it had to be just right. And her bed couldn't be too hard or too soft—it had to be just right. Goldilocks made choices that were based on her personal needs and by making these choices she assumed a stance of autonomy and efficacy. Teachers can help students be like Goldilocks by modeling how to make just-right book selections. The demonstration begins with the teacher describing *too hard, too easy,* and *just right* by showing exemplar books. Teachers might begin by saying,

A "too hard" book is one you would really like to read—perhaps one your big brother or sister has read or one I've read aloud to the class.

But you know it's too difficult for you right now. That's okay. You can pull it out every once in a while to see if it is getting easier. If it is getting easier, what's happening to you? Right! You're getting to be a better reader! Sometimes it might be just a few months before you'll be able to read it better; but sometimes it might be years. (Ohlhausen & Jepson, 1992, p. 34)

After saying this, the teacher might read from a difficult book to demonstrate how she struggles with this too-hard text.

Next the teacher describes too-easy books. Again, the teacher tells the students,

"Too easy" books are old favorites. They're books you like to read for fun and for independent reading times like SSR. They're ones you might decide to pick up and read when you need a break from hard books, when you're feeling kind of low, or when you just need a "good read." Often it's a book you've read before, or one you've practiced reading lots of times. It doesn't always have to be a story book; it can be a magazine, newspaper, joke book, comic book, or nonfiction book. (Ohlhausen & Jepson, 1992, p. 35)

At this point, the teacher illustrates what a too-easy book is by reading a picture book and explaining that it is an old favorite that she still enjoys reading, even though it is too easy.

Finally, the teacher explains a just-right book. To do this the teacher might say the following:

"Just right" books are books you want to read. A "just right" book is one that isn't too difficult—one or two words per page that you don't know. You can use this book to help you to learn to read by practicing the strategies you've been learning. After you've learned to read it really well, then maybe you'll be able to change it to a "too easy" book. (Ohlhausen & Jepson, 1992, p. 35)

The Goldilocks Principle provides a useful example of how teachers can teach students to select books that allow students to read accurately, fluently, and with understanding. This practice is motivating and nurtures student independence, efficacy, and autonomy in reading.

Another strategy for helping students choose books that match their interest and reading level is the rule of thumb method—also known as "sticky palm and greasy fingers" (Reutzel & Cooter, 1992). Students are asked to open a book to any page and begin reading. As they read, students hold up one finger for each word that is unfamiliar. If all five fingers are up at the end of one page, then that text is too difficult. Similarly, if students are holding no fingers up, the book is too easy. The selection is probably just right if they are only holding up two or three fingers.

A third way to match students to text is to use leveled reading material. Leveled books are categorized according to reading difficulty. The difficulty of leveled text is organized along a continuum with levels labeled with a letter from A to Z. Letter designations correlate to grade levels K through eight and provide a continuum of progress for students (Fountas & Pinnell, 2001). These levels are used to match students with independent and instructional reading materials. "There is no way for a student to reach grade level without starting the teaching where the student is" (Fountas & Pinnell, 2001, p. 229).

Several factors are considered when leveling text: length; layout; subject; structure and organization of text; illustrations; words; phrases, sentences, and paragraphs; punctuation; and literary features. Figure 2.3 provides additional information about how these factors influence text leveling (Johnson, 2003). An understanding of how these factors correspond to text difficulty will help teachers guide student text selection. At each level, these factors are analyzed to determine how text features support or challenge readers. Teachers who understand the factors will not have to rely solely on text leveling lists. Also, by knowing the factors, teachers can guide students to independently self-select texts that are appropriate.

Much more needs to be considered when choosing appropriate texts for students. A student's level of knowledge influences the level of text that is appropriate. For example, an appropriate text about spiders for one student might be a below grade level text. For the same student, an appropriate text on dinosaurs might be an above grade level text. If the student has more background knowledge and greater interest in dinosaurs and greater experience reading about dinosaurs, then the student has a more developed vocabulary about dinosaurs. Prior knowledge, interest, and previous reading experience with a topic may enable a student to read a more difficult text.

HOW CAN WE USE ASSESSMENTS TO PERSONALIZE READING INSTRUCTION?

The purpose of literacy assessment is to provide teachers with information to plan and deliver instruction. Assessment permeates every school day and tells us what students have learned, are learning, and are ready to learn (Afflerbach, 1999). It allows us to personalize instruction and starts with getting to know students' attitudes, interests, and preferences (Worthy et al., 2001). This seamless connection between assessment and literacy instruction requires teachers to use a variety of assessments that help identify the most appropriate instruction, independent work, and materials. Assessments that are embedded in ongoing reading and writing do not take time from instruction; rather, they become part of instruction. Figure 2.4 presents a rationale and a variety of strategies and tools for assessing eight areas of student preferences, needs, progress, and strengths: (1) attitudes, interests, and preferences; (2) level of reading; (3) amount, type, and quality of reading; (4) word recognition strengths and needs; (5) comprehension strengths and needs; (6) vocabulary strengths and needs; (7) fluency strengths and needs; and (8) written or oral response to reading.

Figure 2.3 Factors Considered in Leveling Books

Factor	Description
Length	• How many words are in the book? • How many lines of text are on each page? • How many pages are in the book?
Layout	• What size is the print? • How much space is there between words and lines? • What is the relationship between print and illustrations? • Do all sentences begin on the left or do they "wrap around" so that end punctuation must be relied upon? • Is print placed in standard, predictable places on the pages or is it used in creative ways that require the reader's flexibility? • Do size and shape of the book, binding, and layout play a role in text interpretation?
Subject	• Are the concepts or topics familiar to most children? • How many different ideas, topics, characters, or events are included?
Structure and organization of the text	• Are there repeating episodes that help the reader predict story events? • Is there repetitive language? • Are events and information organized chronologically or in some other way? • Are characters' thoughts and actions presented directly or through inference?
Illustrations	• How much picture support for text is there? • Do the pictures help readers understand the text? • Do illustrations help readers interpret the text or go beyond the text?
Words	• Is there a variety of words used to express the same idea or thing as for example, *cried, exclaimed,* or *replied* for *said*? • Are there many multisyllabic words or specialized content words? • Are there many words that are infrequently used in oral language? • Are there many high-frequency words?
Phrases, sentences, paragraphs	• Are there complex sentences joined by *and, but,* or other conjunctions? • Are there complex sentences with embedded clauses? • Are paragraphs organized so that readers can recognize lead sentences and main ideas?
Punctuation	• What variety of punctuation is there? • To what degree must punctuation be used to understand sentence syntax? • To what degree must punctuation be used to understand meaning?
Literary features	• Is character development essential to the story? • How essential to the story are understandings about setting and plot? • Are there literary devices, such as flashbacks or stories within stories that add complexity? • Does the writer use metaphor or other literary devices?

16 THE LEARNING
COMMUNITIES
GUIDE TO
IMPROVING
READING
INSTRUCTION

● **Figure 2.4**   Elements of Literacy Assessment

What Do You Need to Know About Your Students?	Rationale	How Can You Find Out?
Attitudes, interests, and preferences	• To determine what motivates students • To connect text to student interests • To personalize instruction • To identify attitudes and preferences that may support or thwart reading • To determine prior experiences and/or reading history of readers	• Student literacy surveys or questionnaires • Student interviews (teacher or student led) • Observations of students • Parent interviews and surveys
Level of reading	• To match text to student reading ability • To group students for guided reading and literature circle groups • To identify appropriate independent reading material • To provide evidence of progress	• Running records • Informal reading inventories • Miscue analysis • Observation
Amount, type, and quality of reading	• To ensure that students read varied genres • To determine and encourage reading frequency, particularly for reluctant readers • To monitor independent reading	• Reading lists in portfolios • Reading logs • Journal entries • Observation and checklists of students' reading • Contributions to book clubs • Student interviews
Word recognition strengths and needs	• To determine word-solving strategies • To identify skill needs for phonemic awareness, phonics, letter identification, spelling, word recognition, and so on	• Reading word lists • Writing samples • Listening to students read • Oral reading inventories • Miscue analysis from running records or informal reading inventories
Comprehension strengths and needs	• To determine whether students are using the strategies that good readers use to comprehend • To determine if students understand what they read	• Observations of discussions about text • Examination of written responses • Think-aloud analysis • Recording and analyzing retellings • Graphic organizers, Post-it notes, and so on that make students' thinking evident • Formal reading assessments for comprehension

What Do You Need to Know About Your Students?	Rationale	How Can You Find Out?
Vocabulary Strengths and Needs	• To determine deficits pertaining to vocabulary acquisition and use that may impede comprehension	• Choice of words when writing • Multiple-choice tests matching words with meanings, synonyms, or antonyms • Concept definition mapping that requires students to describe what a word is and what it is not, along with examples of use • Semantic feature analysis that requires a student to discern a term's meaning by comparing attributes of other terms that fall into the same category or class • Informal observation of students' word choice and use during conferences, book club conversations, and individual and group discussions
Fluency Strengths and Needs	• To determine whether and how fluency may impede or support comprehension • To determine readers' phrasing, expression, and rate of reading • To determine students' accuracy while reading appropriately leveled text (90–100% accuracy)	• Informal observation of speed and accuracy while students are reading • Informal reading inventories • Timed tests of speed and accuracy in oral reading • Scores on comprehension tests
Written or Oral Response to Reading	• To determine students' emotional and cognitive responses to reading • To determine strategies students use to comprehend	• Written responses to text • Journal entries • Observation of literature discussions • Observation of reading performance during guided reading • Other observations of students' written and oral responses while reading independently or in groups

Since we have been discussing the importance of matching students with text, let's examine how we can analyze students' reading systematically. Through assessment, we can identify the particular reading challenges each student faces so instruction can "accelerate student progress" (Worthy et al., 2001, p. 39). We can assess students' level of reading by using running records or miscue analysis. Running records are used to analyze students' oral reading and may be used on any text the student is reading (Fountas & Pinnell, 2001). The student reads aloud and the teacher records the reading by checking the words read correctly and by coding the words that are read incorrectly, or the miscues. Running records are most appropriate for primary grade students or struggling readers in the upper grades. Because most upper grade students develop speed and fluency, it is difficult to keep up with their reading and record miscues.

Miscue analysis is another assessment to determine challenges to students' reading and can be used to personalize reading instruction. This assessment method analyzes students' reading and processing of text and provides specific information on the students' reading ability. This is a particularly good strategy for teachers to use at the beginning of the school year. Figure 2.5 briefly summarizes the procedures for what is done before, during, and after a miscue analysis. For in-depth information about how to conduct miscue analysis, running records, and informal reading inventories, consult the following sources:

- Clay, M. M. (1993). *An observation survey of early literacy achievement.* Portsmouth, NH: Heinemann.

- Flynt, E. S., & Cooter, R. B. (1999). *English-Espanol reading inventory for the classroom.* Upper Saddle River, NJ: Merrill/Prentice Hall.

- Goodman, K. S. (1969). Analysis of reading miscues: Applied psycholinguistics. *Reading Research Quarterly, 5,* 9–13.

- Leslie, L., & Caldwell, J. (2001). *Qualitative reading inventory-3.* New York: Addison Wesley Longman.

In miscue analysis, it is important to use some kind of abbreviated coding system to record types of errors. Write the error made during oral reading on the copy of the text passage and use codes to represent the type of error. Miscues scored as errors include the following:

- *Substitution:* An incorrect word is substituted and the substitution is written phonetically above the text. This is scored as an error unless the student self-corrects.

- *Insertion:* A word that is not in the text passage is recorded by writing the word above the point where the reader inserted it.

- *Omission:* The reader leaves out a word and this miscue is recorded by circling the omitted word.

- *Teacher Tells:* If the student is stumped, the teacher tells the word after waiting 4–5 seconds and writes the "told" word over the word in the passage with "T" beside it.

⦿ **Figure 2.5**   Before, During, and After Miscue Analysis

Phase	Procedures for Using Miscue Analysis in Oral Reading
Before	• Select an appropriate passage from the beginning of a trade book or basal that is 100–200 words long and write the number of words on the text. • Make a copy of the selected text for the student and set up a tape recorder if you want an audio recording of the reading. • Find a quiet area of the room. • Introduce the text by asking the student to look at the cover and predict what the book will be about. Tell the student you will be listening to him read aloud and will take notes. Inform the student you will ask him about what he read after reading.
During	• Use copies of the text to record errors while the student reads from the text. • Listen to the student read without assisting. • Record all errors, attempts, and self-corrections above the relevant words on the text copy.
After	• Assess comprehension by asking the student to tell about what he just read. • Assist with prompting the student's retelling only if the student struggles. • Discuss miscues with the student and ask if they made sense or should have been corrected. • Ask the student to define one or two key vocabulary words. • Summarize the reader's confidence, expression, and speed (Fountas & Pinnell, 2001; Worthy et al., 2001).

There are some miscues that are not scored but are recorded on the text passage. Recording these miscues provides valuable information on the degree of fluency and confidence. The errors that do not count against the student's score are repetitions, self-corrections, and pauses.

- *Repetitions:* The student reads the word or words more than once and this is recorded with a wavy line under the word or words.

- *Self-corrections:* The reader says a word incorrectly but goes back and self-corrects the error. This is recorded by writing the incorrect word(s) above the word with code "SC."

- *Pauses:* Mark the passage with a slash when the student pauses for more than a second.

Figure 2.6 presents a sample passage that illustrates the different types of miscues that can be made on oral reading assessments and how the miscues are

Figure 2.6   Sample Miscue Analysis

Errors Marked on the Text	# of Errors	Type of Error
Fŏb Phoebe soon settled into her job. The work wasn't as	2	Fob/Phobe (substitution)
hard as she thought it would be. Mrs. Washington had	1	(Accurate reading)
her _Fŏbs_ brought her own quilts and feather beds. It was Phoebe's	1	Substitution, Repetition
job to air and turn these every morning , as well as to see		(Accurate reading)
to the buying of food and (the) serving of meals. She had	1	Omission
clean to keep the silver cleaned and shining and the furniture	1	Substitution
job dusted and polished. She did not have any special jobs to	1	Substitution
do for General Washington, except to see that his meals		Repetition
were served on time. He was very particular about		(Accurate reading)
his _sc_ having dinner served (promptly) at four o'clock, and	1	Insertion, Self-correction
Phoebe sometimes had a hard time getting everything		
finished by then.		(Accurate reading)
General Washington never said (very) much. He was	1	Omission
_Quick_sc_ tall, with a quiet voice. He looked like the kind of man		Self-correction
who could win a war. Mrs. Washington was to have a		(Accurate reading)
pŏmp fresh egg each day, and Pompey, who was a lot of	1	Substitution
Fŏb _year/sc_ company to Phoebe even though he was only eight years		Repetition, Self-correction
old, helped by visiting the hen (early) every morning.	1	Omission
Fŏb When dinner was over, he and Phoebe often stood on the		
told kitchen steps and fed the hens left over scraps of bread	1	Told
from the table.		(Accurate reading)
Number of words: 199 Number of miscues: 11 Percentage of words read correctly: 94% (borderline)		_Fairly slow but attempts sounded right, made sense, and student monitored reading. Retelling included important information._

recorded on the text passage. The passage is presented in the left column, with the student's miscues handwritten above the text. The middle column identifies the number of errors that are counted or scored. Note that some errors are scored while others are not scored but are marked. The right column specifies the type of miscues made.

Analyzing the sample oral reading assessment, we find that the student's miscues were similar to the correct words in the passage. The student left off endings of words a couple of times and omitted three little words but may have made these errors because of concentrating on reading ahead. To calculate the score, the number of miscues (11) is subtracted from the total number of words in the passage (199) to get the number of words read correctly (188). The total number of words read correctly is divided by the number of words in the passage to get the percentage of words read correctly, or a word recognition score of

◉ Figure 2.7   Independent, Instructional, and Frustration Levels of Reading

Level	Definition	Percentage of Correct Words	Retelling Criteria
Independent	The grade level of material that is easy for a student to read with minimal word-recognition errors and with high comprehension.	98–100	Elaborate, no probing necessary
Instructional	The reading level of material that is challenging but not frustrating for the student to read successfully with teacher support.	95–97	Includes the big ideas with a little probing
Frustration	The level of material that is too difficult for a student to read successfully even with instructional support. Comprehension is poor.	Below 90	No details or ideas included

94% (188 ÷ 199 = 94%). This is a borderline score and falls just below the commonly accepted 95% word recognition accuracy desired for the instructional level of reading. Additionally, although the errors did not impact comprehension of the passage significantly, the teacher had to probe for details for the retelling and described comprehension as adequate. This student will need significant support from the teacher to read this particular trade book accurately, fluently, and with understanding and will need easier text to improve reading. Figure 2.7 presents the criteria for analyzing a student's level of reading based on word recognition and comprehension or retelling (Harris & Hodges, 1995; Worthy et al., 2001).

WHAT ARE SOME ADDITIONAL WAYS TO PERSONALIZE READING INSTRUCTION?

The use of rich and varied literature that invites students to read accurately, fluently, and with understanding is the foundation for personalizing reading instruction. Teachers can build differentiated instruction around varied text to develop students' literary skills and understanding. One way is to identify a curricular standard that students at a given grade level are expected to master and develop adjusted learning experiences. These experiences are designed to provide additional scaffolding to emerging learners or expand learning of

22 THE LEARNING
COMMUNITIES
GUIDE TO
IMPROVING
READING
INSTRUCTION

Figure 2.8 Sample Adjusted Learning Experience

Standard/Indicators: **Literary Text** (1) Determine theme and whether it is implied or stated directly. (2) Explain how an author's choice of words appeals to the senses and suggests mood. (3) Identify figurative language in literary works, including idioms, similes, and metaphors.

Group	Students	Demonstrated Knowledge	Targeted Learning Experience
Emerging		• Has difficulty identifying theme • Does not understand mood • Needs "look fors" to help identify theme • Does not see how images suggest possible moods and possible themes • Has difficulty with graphic organizers	Using reading material appropriate to the reader and a graphic organizer provided by the teacher, identify images that are suggested by an author and the words that depict these images.
Meeting		• Can identify theme most of the time • Doesn't see the relationship between key words, mood, images, and themes • Can use graphic organizers when directed	Using reading material appropriate to the reader and a graphic organizer provided by the teacher, examine figurative language and theme in an author's literary work by identifying key words, feelings, symbols/images, structure, and theme.
Exceeding		• Is consistent in identifying theme • Is proficient with using graphic organizers • Is proficient with types of figurative language	Create a graphic organizer to compare, contrast, and reflect an author's use of various types of figurative language to depict theme in two literary works.

students who have demonstrated mastery of the targeted standard. Adjusted learning experiences are based on an initial assessment of students that provides information about what they already know or can do relative to standards. Figure 2.8 describes sample adjusted learning experiences that focus on particular standards about theme, mood, and figurative language. Note that the teacher "unpacks" the standard for emerging learners who need additional support because they do not have a clear understanding of theme, much less mood. This is accomplished by using a graphic organizer that helps students see the connection between images and words. On the other hand, the teacher knows there are also some students who have a clear understanding of theme, mood, and figurative language and wants those students to stretch by looking at how particular authors use figurative language. Additionally there is the group of students who are performing at grade level and are meeting the standards fairly easily. This group of students understands theme but needs help examining how words, feelings, symbolism or imagery, and features of text can aid in identifying themes.

To personalize reading instruction, teachers can immerse students in literature by implementing varied learning experiences that reflect different learning styles, strengths, and multiple intelligences. Considering learning styles, strengths, and multiple intelligences moves us from a deficit focus on student weaknesses to a more positive focus on student strengths and interests. By incorporating various techniques for having students learn and process information, we come closer to providing brain-compatible classrooms where learning thrives and diversity is honored.

In his seminal work *Frames of Mind: The Theory of Multiple Intelligences* (1983), Howard Gardner advanced the idea that learners have varied ways of processing information and he labeled these different ways *intelligences.* We include a description of the eight intelligences and how they might be applied to reading instruction as an alternative way to personalize reading instruction. By getting to know students' strengths in learning, teachers can design learning experiences that consider the students they teach. Eight intelligences have been identified:

1. *Visual/spatial:* visual depiction of information and ideas through imagining, visualizing, and seeing in the minds eye

2. *Verbal/linguistic:* language and literacy through reading, writing, speaking, and listening

3. *Logical/mathematical:* ability to reason and think in abstractions through debating, calculating, computing, and concluding

4. *Musical/rhythmic:* sense of melody, rhythm, and rhyme

5. *Bodily/kinesthetic:* muscle memory of the body through hands-on learning, manipulatives, lab work, and practicums

6. *Interpersonal/social:* skills of caring, comforting, collaborating, and communicating through team tasks, group activities, and partner work

7. *Intrapersonal/introspective:* ability to be self-aware, self-regulating, and self-assessing through learning logs, response journals, goal setting, and personal portfolios

8. *Naturalist/physical world:* ability to see the natural world through the lens of a scientist by classifying, observing, analyzing, and seeing the relationships between natural phenomena (Fogarty, 2002, pp. 198–199).

24 THE LEARNING
COMMUNITIES
GUIDE TO
IMPROVING
READING
INSTRUCTION

These intelligences are entry points for the learner. Teachers can facilitate learning by providing students with varied ways to process information (Fogarty, 2002, p. 196). For example, some learners learn best by interacting with others (interpersonal/social intelligence), while others learn by using their bodies or physical manipulation (bodily/kinesthetic intelligence). Also, by incorporating several intelligences into a learning experience, teachers can help students access different active learning pathways that will enhance literary understanding. Figure 2.9 provides a sample lesson designed to have students learn vocabulary words pertaining to Thomas Jefferson and government. As can be seen, the learning experience integrates an English and social studies standard using informational text. From this informational text, teachers have identified key vocabulary words the students need to know. All students will learn the same words in cooperative groups but will learn in different ways. The teacher can either have students choose which way they want to learn the words or can assign students to a group based on intelligence strength or weakness. For example, the teacher may want some students to develop a way of learning and other students to use preferred ways of knowing. However the teacher determines groups, students will be actively engaged in learning vocabulary, and this active engagement is crucial to improving reading, writing, and speaking.

Figure 2.9 Sample Vocabulary Lesson Using Multiple Intelligences

Standard(s): The student will read and learn the meanings of unfamiliar words (English).

The student will identify the contributions that Virginians made to the establishment of the U.S. Constitution and the success of the new national government (Social Studies).

Intelligences	Students	Targeted Learning Experience
• Bodily/ kinesthetic • Interpersonal/ social • Verbal/linguistic		• Provide list of vocabulary words for reading informational text about Thomas Jefferson's role in establishing government for the United States. • Students will work in cooperative groups to determine definitions of the words. • Students will develop a bodily kinesthetic representation for each of the words in cooperatives groups. • Students will pair up to take turns providing a bodily kinesthetic representation and vocabulary word definitions when one member of the pair calls out a vocabulary word. • The group will teach the bodily kinesthetic representation to other class members.
• Musical/ rhythmic • Interpersonal/ social		• Provide list of vocabulary words for reading informational text about Thomas Jefferson's role in establishing government for the United States.

Intelligences	Students	Targeted Learning Experience
• Verbal/linguistic		• Students will work in cooperative groups to determine definitions of the words. • Students will develop a rhythmic presentation or jingle of the vocabulary words and their meanings in cooperative groups. This can be in either song or rap form. • The group will present their rhythmic product to the class.
• Visual/spatial • Interpersonal/ social • Verbal/linguistic		• Provide list of vocabulary words for reading informational text about Thomas Jefferson's role in establishing government for the United States. • Students will work in cooperative groups to determine definitions of the words. • Students will create a word game for identifying the vocabulary words. • Students will demonstrate how the word game is played.

WHAT WERE THE BIG IDEAS IN THIS CHAPTER?

Chapter 2 describes the importance of personalizing reading instruction and presents four broad considerations for differentiation: environment, content, process, and product. We examined how to hook students on literature by tapping into their interests and learning preferences. We scrutinized the link between student motivation, attitude, efficacy, and reading materials and found that just-right texts are crucial to helping students read, write, and discuss at higher levels of comprehension. We considered how to level text and how to guide students' self-selection of text. Additionally, we found ways to personalize instruction by creating adjustable learning assignments. Finally, we delved into the seamless connection between literacy assessment and literacy instruction. Personalizing instruction means we collect information about our students in eight areas: (1) attitudes, interests, and preferences; (2) level of reading; (3) amount, type, and quality of reading; (4) word recognition strengths and needs; (5) comprehension strengths and needs; (6) vocabulary strengths and needs; (7) fluency strength and needs; and (8) written or oral response to reading. In particular, we looked at how miscue analysis can be used to gain information about our students.

26 THE LEARNING
COMMUNITIES
GUIDE TO
IMPROVING
READING
INSTRUCTION

CONSTRUCTIVE REFLECTION

As a professional learning team, choose one of the following reflections to apply key concepts presented in Chapter 2.

1. Choose a child in your classroom for a case study and apply some of the strategies described in this chapter to gather information about this student's interests, preferences, and reading level. Develop a plan to personalize instruction for this child and share the data you collected, as well as the plan with your teaching team. Study, plan, and share (a) student interests, (b) learning preferences, (c) reading level, (d) strengths and weaknesses, and (e) methods used to gather this information.

2. Review the four-corner framework for differentiating literacy instruction (Figure 2.1). Make a written commitment to achieve one concrete goal in each of the four corners using the graphic organizer below (Figure 2.10). Share your goals and your progress toward achieving your goals with a colleague.

Figure 2.10   Goal Setting in the Four Corners of Differentiated Instruction

ENVIRONMENT GOAL	CONTENT GOAL
PROCESS GOAL	PRODUCT GOAL

Managing Environments for Literacy 3

Imagine this . . .

You wonder if the other teachers on your team see you as disorganized as you feel. As a first-year teacher, you recently implemented some small group instruction but feel frustrated with your attempts. For one thing, it seems that when you work with a guided reading group, many of the other students wander around the classroom. You also notice that those who do work seem bored. Students constantly interrupt you while you provide small group instruction. They ask, "What do we do next?" At times the noise level is so loud you can't hear yourself speak. The classroom library you are supposed to have is not used because students can't find appropriate reading materials. You know that you must get some help so you talked with your literacy coach. She invited you to come and observe how she organized her classroom. She wants you to focus on responding to four key questions: (1) How do the daily schedule and agenda support teaching reading and writing? (2) How are various grouping options used to accommodate teaching and learning? (3) How is the classroom library and room organized to engage students? (4) What are other students doing when the teacher is working with a small group of students?

Do the questions this first-year teacher asked sound familiar? Our experience is that many teachers struggle with how to organize their classrooms to support student engagement in reading, writing, and talking about literature. It's a given that we need to provide small group instruction at times to help all students achieve at higher levels, but engaging students in meaningful literacy work while we work with small groups is a significant challenge. Issues of environment and management are linked inextricably to issues of instruction and achievement. In fact, classroom management wields the greatest influence on student achievement (Wang, Haertel, & Walberg, 1993).

Think about a time when you participated in a learning experience that was disorganized. Could you have learned more if the experience was more organized? Were you unsure of the expectations that the person facilitating the experience had for you? Were you frustrated? The truth is that environment or management either supports learning or discourages learning, and this is particularly true of something as complex as reading.

What do we mean by environment? Environmental theorists help us understand how inclusive the concept of environment is. Environmental theory maintains that "the totality of external things, conditions, and influences, including instruction, can facilitate literacy development" (Harris & Hodges, 1995, p. 73). When viewed in this light, environment has to do with prevailing interpersonal relationships, instructional experiences, organizing materials, time, students, routine tasks, and classroom set-up. Exemplary teachers of reading do not experience frequent student discipline problems because they incorporate student-directed teaching and active student engagement. Research supports what our experiences reveal: Student achievement, discipline, and instruction are codependent partners in effective literacy classrooms. Thus, we devoted Chapter 4 to "Ensuring Student Engagement" and Chapter 5 to "Emphasizing Active Teaching." This chapter is devoted to examining other environmental aspects that affect teaching and learning literacy.

WHAT DO STUDENTS NEED FROM A LITERACY LEARNING ENVIRONMENT?

High levels of learning ". . . can only occur when children are working in nonthreatening, emotionally supportive environments with teachers who have high expectations that the children will learn and that they can teach them" (Lyons, 2003, p. 172).

Our students come to us with varied backgrounds, support systems, and experiences. Regardless of our students' background and experiences, what we do with our students will either promote or thwart their beliefs in themselves as learners of literacy. Indeed, student-teacher social interactions play a bigger role in student learning than do student-teacher academic interactions (Wang et al., 1993). Furthermore, when we look at the lives of resilient children—that is, students who achieve in school despite less than supportive home environments—we find the presence of one person in their lives who serves as a mentor. This mentor communicates to the resilient student, "I believe in you and believe that you can learn, and I will support your learning." A mentor can be any family member, another student, a neighbor, or a teacher who serves as a learning advocate for the student. Therefore, it is important for us to nurture positive teacher-to-student, teacher-to-teacher, teacher-to-administrator, staff-to-parent, and student-to-student interactions. We find that in schools where students thrive, there is a no-excuses attitude and a shared message of urgency that all students will achieve. As one principal articulated,

And so coming every day and doing your job and going home is not enough. 'Cause I think that working hard means having a sense of urgency, having a sense that unless children are performing at a higher level than they were when I saw them at the beginning of the year, unless I'm part of the life of the school, unless I'm contributing inside my classroom and outside in a larger arena of the school, I'm not working as hard as I can work. (Gregory, 2002, p. 96)

We have the power to create robust learning environments for literacy by creating places where students feel safe and are not threatened, feel a sense of accomplishment, and are respected as individuals. Figure 3.1 summarizes

Figure 3.1   Student Needs and Teacher Responses for a Positive Literacy Environment

In positive literacy environments, students . . .	Because teachers . . .
Feel safe and not threatened.	• Do not use sarcasm • Handle inappropriate behavior privately • Discourage bullying • Teach students how to give positive feedback through modeling and explicit teaching • Do not use assessment to "zap" students • Use predominately formative assessments, instead of summative assessments • Create circles of friends
Feel like they belong to a learning community.	• Model that they are also learners in the class learning community • Value diversity and differentiate instruction • Expose students to multicultural literature • Respect the dignity of students • Emphasize collaboration and decrease competition • Involve students in making decisions about key aspects of classroom life • Form flexible instructional groups
Have a sense of responsibility for their learning and the learning of others.	• Communicate high expectations • Monitor student work to ensure that students perform as they should • Read and discuss rich literature with characters that portray responsibility • Create classroom libraries and teach students how to select just-right books
Receive recognition for their accomplishments as readers and writers	• Create places to honor and display student work • Provide specific and positive feedback about what students do well in reading, writing, and talking about literature • Share student work samples during reading and writing mini-lessons • Provide time for students to share their work

(Continued)

30 THE LEARNING
COMMUNITIES
GUIDE TO
IMPROVING
READING
INSTRUCTION

Figure 3.1 (Continued)

In positive literacy environments, students . . .	Because teachers . . .
Engage in literacy tasks that are authentic, relevant, and substantive.	• Base instruction on students' prior knowledge, experiences, and interests • Connect reading and writing to the students' world as much as possible • Integrate teaching of reading and writing across the content areas • Use rich fiction and nonfiction
Know what is expected of them to accomplish literacy tasks at high levels.	• Provide clear, concise, step-by-step directions, in written and auditory form, for completing learning tasks • Use rubrics and exemplars to communicate expectations • Model for students how to be well-organized, prompt, positive, self-directed, and patient
Understand the classroom code of conduct and consequences.	• Engage students in identifying a *brief* list of "guidelines" for classroom behavior • Inform students of standards of acceptable behavior immediately • Develop and use consistent, relevant, and appropriate consequences for guiding behavior • Correct misbehavior before it intensifies or spreads
Use routines to facilitate their work as readers and writers.	• Establish routines for working independently, at centers, in small groups, and whole groups by teaching routines one at a time • Post written directions for routines or work • Develop and use a management system that communicates the schedule and expectations for assigned independent and small group work
Know how to form groups, interact in groups, and handle conflict.	• Teach students group interaction and social skills systematically • Provide opportunities for students to work and get to know all their classroom peers through pairs, literature circles, guided reading groups, center work, etc. • Teach students conflict resolution skills explicitly
Have intrinsic motivation to read and write.	• Create a cheerful, well organized environment with spaces for individual, small group, and whole group instruction • Provide and organize varied tools and materials that promote effective, independent readers and writers • Permit student choice with respect to what they read and write • Provide easy books for all students in the classroom to read so they can develop a sense of efficacy about themselves as readers • Scaffold instruction appropriately, according to students' strengths and needs

what students need, as well as what we can do to create a positive literacy environment (Bellanca & Fogarty, 2001; Burke, 2000; Dreikurs, 1971; Glasser, 1986; Ivey, 2002; Johnson & Johnson, 1986; Pressley, 2002). This graphic emphasizes how teacher behaviors and actions are related to ten needs of learners. Learners need to: (1) feel safe, (2) feel like they belong, (3) have a sense of responsibility, (4) receive recognition, (5) engage in authentic literacy tasks, (6) know what is expected of them, (7) understand the classroom code of conduct, (8) use routines to facilitate their work, (9) know how to work in groups, and (10) have intrinsic motivation to read and write. The remainder of this chapter presents concrete strategies and examples for addressing each of these ten student needs. Strategies and examples are grouped and presented around use of text materials, grouping practices, time, routines, and classroom set-up.

WHAT TYPES OF TEXTS SUPPORT RICH LITERACY ENVIRONMENTS?

Have you ever peeked into a classroom when nobody was there? If so, did you make any assumptions about the teacher's instructional values and practices or the students' daily routines? If an anthropologist peeked into your classroom, what assumptions do you think would be made about you and your teaching? Would the anthropologist see student-made books, photographs of favorite books exhibited, class-constructed charts, word walls, boxes of trade books at all levels, and portfolios of writing in progress? When we study classroom literacy we assess the interaction among reading materials, students, and classroom environment and we observe what people do with literacy (Hoffman, 2003). The study of classroom literacy is the study of text and how text is used in a classroom. It involves more than counting the number of texts. A snapshot of literacy in a classroom focuses on the use of texts and how they are valued and understood by both students and teachers.

The school library has moved from a single location to all classrooms in some schools. In high achieving classrooms, teachers' collections of books average about 120 trade books per student, and 70% of those books are bought by teachers (Hoffman, 2003). This is in stark contrast to reality: Hoffman generally found an average of only 31 trade books per student. Lower gains in comprehension were associated with classrooms where basal textbooks served as the primary books that students read. This compelling research has important implications for establishing classroom environments conducive to high quality reading and writing. Classrooms with significant quantities of trade books, authentic texts, and class-constructed texts achieve higher student engagement and higher student motivation to read.

The need for quality classroom libraries and print-rich environments is critical when we consider the diverse students we teach. Many of our students come to school possessing a sense of efficacy about themselves as readers and many do not. In part, this sense of efficacy is related to whether they grow up in a print-rich and language-rich environment surrounded by adults who read and talk about what they read. We know that many students live in homes without a single book, and the result is that these students practice reading less. A deficit of print materials also means these students come to school with less background knowledge and less development of reading competencies needed for high-level comprehension (Pressley, 2002). This poor-getting-poorer and rich-getting-richer phenomena in reading (Stanovich, 1986) has devastating effects on our low-socioeconomic students. These students need extensive classroom libraries to stop this cycle. "Children must have easy—literally fingertip—access to books that provide engaging, successful reading experiences throughout the calendar year if we want them to read in volume" (Allington & McGill-Franzen, 2003, p. 74).

Reading in volume is essential for struggling students to catch up. Exemplary classroom environments include a wide variety of texts that are organized for easy access by students. Classroom libraries are stocked with extensive nonfiction and fiction trade books about a wide range of topics and on a wide range of levels. Books organized for easy access by students may be stored in plastic bins and grouped. A variety of categories may be used to group books for easy access and include the following:

- Topics

- Themes

- Genres

- Content areas (science, social studies, mathematics, art, music, etc.)

- Favorite authors

- Book series

- Difficulty levels

Also, teachers can create table-top or desktop reading boxes that contain appropriately leveled reading materials for groups of students. When not working with the teacher, students select books from their box, read silently at their independent level, and practice reading strategies. Teachers can place students' names on laminated index cards taped to each box. Additionally, response-to-reading prompts on standard index cards stimulate student reflection and journal writing.

One of the most valued types of text is the classroom-generated text: texts generated collaboratively by students and teachers. These classroom texts provide a rich medium and scaffolding for literacy development. Literature comes alive in classrooms where the teacher and students are authors of original text and where class texts are displayed in every corner and every available space. Such exhibits of classroom text communicate, "We are a community of readers and writers—we are not just consumers of text—we are generators of text."

Students and teachers in exemplary classrooms generate and read a wide variety of texts. These texts range from class books to laminated poems on chart paper to word walls that grow around the room. The variety should include

- Class books about topics the class is studying or places they have been
- Illustrated books that reflect select authors' writing styles
- Editing charts
- Inquiry charts that reflect student questions about topics they are investigating
- Class rubrics
- Poetry
- "Word walls" that provide a growing list of words students use in writing.

HOW DO WE GROUP STUDENTS FOR READING AND WRITING AT HIGH LEVELS?

Grouping is another consideration for personalizing or differentiating literacy instruction. Exemplary teachers consider and use a wide variety of grouping options and provide small group instruction more frequently than less accomplished teachers (Taylor & Pearson, 2002). Grouping options move along a continuum from individual to whole class and may include pairs and flexible small groups of students. We group to honor students' strengths and needs in the learning process. In brief, grouping meets students' need for "knowledge, power, and affection" (Nagel, 2001, p. 32).

A primary reason for grouping is that it increases student achievement. Grouping is not synonymous with tracking, which keeps students in fixed groups over time with little chance to move ahead. Instead, flexible grouping does the following:

- Extends knowledge and provides appropriate levels of challenge
- Allows student choice and pursuit of what is interesting and important to them
- Nurtures collaboration and a learning community
- Promotes increased active engagement by individual students
- Facilitates management of instruction, materials, and resources
- Allows for in-depth teacher-directed instruction
- Provides opportunities for observation and assessment (New Zealand Ministry of Education, 1997).

Students can be grouped in a number of ways, and grouping is particularly useful in integrating reading and writing across the content areas. Figure 3.2 provides a template to guide teachers' considerations about grouping. Effective grouping considers (1) what is taught, (2) why students should be grouped, (3) the nature of the group, (4) how students are assigned to groups, (5) how group work will be differentiated, and (6) how group work will be assessed. A discussion of each consideration follows.

What are you going to teach? It is appropriate to provide whole group instruction when the whole class, regardless of reading levels, needs to learn certain strategies, skills, or concepts. For example, you may plan a read aloud during which you will introduce and model questioning as a comprehension strategy. Because this is a learning experience that the whole class needs, small group instruction is not necessary. Also, whole group work can build class community through sharing poetry, choral reading, singing, and performing plays.

Why do you think you need to group? As mentioned earlier, students benefit from grouping for a variety of reasons. When content or material is too difficult or too easy for some, it is time to employ grouping. Also, we may feel a need to hook students' learning through a particular lens of interest. Let's build off the example provided earlier. After modeling and giving direct instruction on the comprehension strategy of questioning, you decide you want students to practice this strategy in self-selected books. You group students together based on interest in particular topics and give each group a bin of leveled texts about those topics. As the small groups read their leveled books, they use sticky notes to record their questions. Natural conversation about books flows because each student in the small group reads about the same topic in different leveled books and they develop questioning as a comprehension strategy.

How do you want to group your students? Flexible grouping alternatives prevail in literacy classrooms that encourage students to read and write at high levels. Most of the options listed in Figure 3.2 are self-explanatory; however, a few may need further description. *Multiple intelligences* is a grouping option that engages students in a particular way of learning. This grouping method is referred to in Chapter 2, where a sample lesson plan is provided. Grouping based on a common *interest in favorite authors* motivates students as they read a series of books and study the author's writing style. *Point-of-view* groups emerge when reading material could be viewed from several perspectives. For example, when reading informational text about internment of Japanese citizens during World War II, students could be grouped to discuss what was read from various points-of-view. Another grouping option is to have students work in small groups that create differentiated projects about a topic. Expanding on what was read and discussed in small groups about Japanese internment during World War II, students could determine how they will present what they learned from reading. One group may decide to create a PowerPoint presentation, another may write and illustrate their own book about the subject, and yet another may decide to write and perform a Readers Theater.

How will you determine which students will be assigned to each group? In effective literacy classrooms, teachers are not the only ones making decisions about group composition; students can decide about group membership, or it may be determined by chance, using a strategy such as counting-off. When a teacher

Figure 3.2 Considerations for Grouping

THINKING ABOUT GROUPING?	
Considerations for Grouping	**Response**
1. What are you going to teach?	
2. Why you think you need to group?	
3. How will you group your students? Number of groups? Students in each group? **Possibilities:** | Interests	Multiple Intelligences
Learning Styles	Products
Points of View	Ability
Skill Needs	Strengths
Author Interest	Books
Heterogenous	Guided reading
Scaffolding	Strategies		
4. How you will determine which students will be assigned to each group?	
5. How will the group work be differentiated? **Example:** 	Emerging	Meeting	Exceeding
?	?	?		
6. How will you determine if each of the groups has accomplished the learning goals?	

36 THE LEARNING
COMMUNITIES
GUIDE TO
IMPROVING
READING
INSTRUCTION

makes a decision about grouping students, it should be based on an informal or formal assessment of students' strengths, needs, interests, and learning preferences. Various informal and formal assessment options are described in Chapter 2.

How will the group work be differentiated? If students are grouped, some kind of differentiation should take place. It may be that differentiation is facilitated because the task is so open-ended that it allows for a differentiated response. For example, the teacher may place students in cooperative, heterogeneous, random groups and ask each group to use the "sketch to stretch" strategy to respond to sections of text (Sejnost & Thiese, 2001). The teacher reads a portion of the text aloud to the class and pauses to let groups discuss what they think is most important about what was read, draw it, and provide a summary. For this learning experience, the groups create different products, yet the teacher also expects to find similar responses across groups. The teacher allows for differentiated responses in group discussions, visuals, and written summary statements but checks all students for expected responses. Group learning experiences also can be differentiated by texts, materials, tasks, or products. Whatever the case, differentiation considers the content being taught, the reason groups were created, the abilities and needs of group members, and the products they create.

How will you determine if each group has accomplished the learning goals? This last consideration for grouping need not be cumbersome, yet assessment is essential to move students forward in reading and writing. Often assessment occurs informally as the teacher observes students working in small groups and takes notes. With the seamless connection that exists between effective literacy instruction and authentic assessment, students usually create products that demonstrate whether and how they accomplish learning goals. Teachers can use interviews, graphic organizers, observations, performance tasks, rubrics, portfolios, work samples, and tape recordings to assess student progress during group work.

HOW IS TIME USED TO PROMOTE HIGH LEVELS OF READING AND WRITING?

Depending on how we use it, time is either our instructional friend or foe. With few exceptions, we all have basically the same amount of time during the school day, yet exemplary teachers somehow allocate more time for students to actively engage in reading, writing, and talking about text than less accomplished teachers do. These teachers have learned that pacing and efficiency are partners in using time wisely; therefore, they follow these time management principles:

- Establish a productive and easy-to-accomplish task that students do every morning as they enter the classroom.

- Take care of routine business quickly.

- Vary the schedule across the week.

- Hold a morning meeting and explain the day's schedule.

- Establish management routines that save time such as journals for reading workshop, portfolios or notebooks for writer's workshop, and designated places for students to put completed work (Fountas & Pinnell, 2001, p. 97).

Regardless of how your school day is structured, the schedule for language arts should include blocks of time for reading workshop, writing workshop, and language/word study. At least one hour is recommended for both reading and writing workshop, and no more than 30 minutes for language/word study. If more time is available for language arts, consider devoting the time to reading workshop. CIERA found that exemplary classrooms spend an average of 125 minutes on reading alone (Taylor, 2003). Moreover, 48 of the 125 minutes is spent on fluency, which includes independent reading and teacher-directed instruction. Out of the 48 minutes spent on fluency, students in exemplary classrooms averaged 33 minutes per day on independent reading. Further, students in exemplary classrooms spent an average of 36 minutes on comprehension, including skills/strategies instruction and talking/writing about text.

In terms of managing time, the best schedule is one that provides a large block of time that can be used flexibly across all three language arts segments. Chapter 5 provides a more in-depth description of what goes on during each block of time. Note that the blocks of time may be expanded by having students engage in independent work that crosses over to another block of time. For example, during reader's workshop, students may work on a writer's notebook for independent work. Also, the blocks of time may be expanded by having students apply what they learn from reader's workshop, writer's workshop, and language/word study to social studies and science.

WHAT ROUTINES CAN BE ESTABLISHED FOR INDEPENDENT AND SMALL GROUP WORK?

Students work best in literacy classrooms where routines and expectations are clearly and consistently communicated. "Every moment invested in teaching routines will save hours of instructional time later" (Fountas & Pinnell, 2001, p. 105). Routines foster self-directed, independent work habits for reading, writing, and talking about text and expand students' learning opportunities. Routines should be taught systematically, and time should be provided for students to practice the routines. Some routines take longer to learn and will require more scaffolding than others. Thus, teachers will want to observe students closely as they apply new routines and gradually release responsibility to students as they demonstrate mastery. To teach routines teachers may wish to consider the following techniques:

38 THE LEARNING
COMMUNITIES
GUIDE TO
IMPROVING
READING
INSTRUCTION

- Introduce one center at a time and model exactly what students should do.

- Model what the students' behavior looks like and sounds like during the routine.

- Model what students do if a problem arises.

- Model how independent work should be completed and submitted.

- Engage students in assessing their independent work.

- Create a management board or some other management system that informs students of their daily literacy responsibilities (Pavelka, 2002).

Teachers often ask us how to organize time to accommodate guided reading, small group, or independent work. We often suggest that teachers daily rotate groups of students with whom they meet and provide more frequent small group instruction for struggling students. Guided reading groups are flexible, and membership changes as students' strengths and needs change. When first attempting to implement guided reading groups, teachers may assign the same literacy task to the remainder of the class—silent reading and journal writing. This allows the teacher to focus on effectively implementing guided reading.

When effective teachers provide multiple independent work opportunities and options for students, they create highly effective and efficient management systems. In some classrooms, teachers use a bulletin board as a management system showing both guided reading groups and independent work. Let's look at what a teacher might include on the management system. First, the teacher would consider the number of guided reading groups that can be managed. Guided reading groups will change in membership as students demonstrate improved reading, need for extra help with a particular genre, need for assistance with particular comprehension strategies, and so on.

With this in mind, a teacher creates four "stellar" guided reading groups named sun, moon, star, and planet (Can you tell the class is studying the solar system?). Figure 3.3 provides a sample chart showing the guided reading group names and the students who are currently part of that group (total of 20 students). This chart is posted on a bulletin board and constantly changes as student needs change. The teacher uses this chart flexibly, so it is laminated without the names of the groups or the students. The teacher changes group names and student names by using index cards hung on hooks attached to each grid of the guided reading group chart.

The teacher also creates a second chart that is posted next to the guided reading group chart. Like the guided reading group chart, the new chart is blank with hooks in each section of the grid so that the teacher can use index cards to indicate changes in group names and group membership (Figure 3.4). As the figure illustrates, the teacher works with two guided reading groups

Figure 3.3   Sample Guided Reading Group Chart

Guided Reading Group	Students
Sun	Sue, Shameka, Jamal, Judy, Pete,
Moon	Brian, Char, Wayne, Tywan, Keisha
Star	Eric, Hosea, Sara, Leah, Akela
Planet	Joan, Leon, Scott, Rosa, Divonne

each day. While she works with these two groups, the other students have assigned tasks and rotate through the six possible activities: writer's notebook, writing center, standards-based center, reader response group, partner reading, and independent reading. The teacher goes over the tasks at the beginning of the week and displays a written explanation on the chart. Note that the Friday schedule is left open so the teacher can decide to work with guided reading groups, provide whole class instruction, or allow student choices to engage in other types of experiences.

Productive independent or small group work in classroom literacy centers focuses on promoting growth in reading and writing. Sometimes center work is completed at the literacy centers and sometimes the work is done at students' desks. A smart approach to initiating centers is to start small, with one center at a time, and slow—implementing successive centers when students work independently and successfully at each center. A small number of centers may support productive, independent work while the teacher conducts small group instruction or conferences with individuals. These centers operate throughout the school year, with students following routines that do not vary. What students read and write varies, but the process or the center work stays the same. In this way, center work is manageable for both students and teachers, not requiring additional work for teachers. Figure 3.5 provides a description of yearlong centers and routines that were included in Figure 3.4.

Record keeping is crucial to sustaining organized literacy environments. Teachers keep records about tasks students complete, books students read, questions students ask, strengths students demonstrate, and problems students encounter. Exemplary teachers also expect students to reflect upon the work they do and maintain records of accomplishments.

The weekly literacy task log (Figure 3.6) is one way teachers can help students reflect upon accomplishments. On a daily basis, teachers give students time to complete the log, citing accomplishments, concerns, and completed tasks. Also, during a whole group wrap-up time, students share something they accomplished, something they are proud of, something they would like to improve, or a question they have. Students keep their weekly literacy task logs in manila folders at a central location so that the teacher can review them periodically.

40 THE LEARNING
COMMUNITIES
GUIDE TO
IMPROVING
READING
INSTRUCTION

◉ **Figure 3.4**

Centers	Description	Monday	Tuesday	Wednesday	Thursday	Friday
Writer's Notebook		Sun	Moon	Star	Planet	• Individuals conference with teacher, • Book clubs or literature circles, • Journal writing, • Word study, & • Computer center.
Writing Center		Moon Planet	Sun Star			
Standard-Based Center		Moon Planet	Sun Star			
Reader Response Group				Moon Planet	Sun Star	
Partner Reading				Moon Planet	Sun Star	
Independent Reading		Sun, Moon, Star, Planet	Sun, Moon, Star, Planet	Sun, Moon, Star, Planet	Sun, Moon, Star, Planet	Sun, Moon, Star, Planet
Guided Reading Group		Sun Star	Moon Planet	Star Sun	Planet Moon	Guided Reading as Needed

HOW IS CLASSROOM SPACE ORGANIZED TO PROMOTE HIGH LEVELS OF READING AND WRITING?

Exemplary literacy classrooms are warm and inviting places that nurture a learning community and a sense of belonging among students. The arrangement of furniture, materials, and centers supports the flow of whole class, small group, and independent work. How the classroom space is organized impacts how quickly and quietly students accomplish their work and how the teacher manages the learning of twenty-five or more students. Teachers may consider arranging seven working areas to promote literacy: (1) whole class meeting space, (2) at least two small group work areas, (3) book area, (4) writing and publishing center, (5) standards-based center, (6) word study area, and (7) social studies/science center. Center spaces should be organized so that students know where to find and return the materials with which they work. Figure 3.7 provides a description of working areas to promote literacy.

◉ Figure 3.5   Description of Yearlong Centers and Routines

Center	Description of Center
Independent reading	Independent reading is the most important routine, and students can read silently in the class library, at their desks, or on a rug. Students keep journals or reading logs in which they record what they read and their responses to those books.
Independent writer's notebook	Students record and collect ideas, questions, and notes on topics they want to learn about in their writer's notebook. Their writer's notebook is a resource of possible topics for independent writing and a collection of favorite author's words, phrases or sentences that they want to remember (Fletcher, 1996, Fountas & Pinnell, 2001).
Partner reading	Pairs choose and read texts that are at their independent reading level and may include texts that the teacher has read aloud in shared reading, texts from classroom libraries, and texts practiced in guided reading.
Reader response group	Students meet as a "background group" as an extension of guided reading (Pavelka, 2002). The background group sits in close proximity to the guided reading group but works independently of the teacher. This way the teacher may watch and monitor the group. The teacher organizes boxes or plastic tubs of leveled texts from which students choose a set of the same book to read and talk about. Students list the titles of the books they are reading and write about what they have read in response to teacher-generated questions such as, What do you think will happen next in the story? What is the big idea? What is your favorite part? What other book does this remind you of? Did anything like this ever happen to you?
Writing center	Writing materials are organized for easy access for individual, paired, and small group writing. The writing center can include the following: a table and chairs, easels and bulletin boards for exhibiting writing, writing materials (a variety of markers and paper), portfolios or folders for organizing writing samples, and a message board for class members to use.
Standards-based centers (Cassetta, 2001)	The center provides explicit directions for students to follow in responding to a book they are reading. These instructions can focus on developing literary skills that are common to state standards such as theme, plot, setting, and character analysis. This center provides independent practice for standard assessments. One or two graphic organizers or rubrics are created for each of the standards. For example, the books students read change, but they respond to the same graphic organizer for theme throughout the year. Teachers can ask students to present their work to the whole class as a way of sharing what they are reading with others.

Figure 3.6   Weekly Literacy Task Log

WEEKLY LITERACY TASK LOG					
Student:			**Date of Log:**		
Task	*Monday*	*Tuesday*	*Wednesday*	*Thursday*	*Friday*
I read this text . . .					
I independently read . . .					
I partner read (list title and partner)					
I wrote and/or published . . .					
I did the graphic organizer for this standard . . .					
During guided reading I . . .					
I did this in my writer's notebook . . .					
The work I am most proud of is . . .					
Something I would like to improve is . . .					
A question I have is . . .					

Figure 3.7 Description of Working Areas to Promote Literacy

Working Area	Description of Components
1. Whole class meeting space	• A large enough space for the entire class to meet together • A rocking chair for the teacher to sit in while reading aloud/providing instruction • A rug for students to sit on • A chart stand, easel, or bulletin board
2. Two small group work areas	• Space to accommodate four to six students for guided reading/writing, literature study, mini lessons, background groups, and so on • Enough table top space for four to six students • Four to six student chairs and a chair for the teacher • An area in the center of the room and another in a corner of the room with high visibility from each small group meeting area
3. Book area	• Guidelines for using book area and checking out books for home use • Attractively displayed books • Plastic tubs that organize and classify books • Shelving and space for organizing books • Headsets and taped stories • Story manipulatives such as felt boards, puppets, and materials for constructing felt stories • Labeled plastic tubs indicating book categories • A couch, several comfortable chairs, and cushions • A home-like environment • The bulk of the classroom books (also have books in other parts of the room)
4. Writing and publishing center	• Guidelines for using writing and publishing center • A table, chairs, charts, and bulletin board for writing display • Labeled containers for writing and illustration supplies such as different kinds of writing paper, different types of writing utensils, markers, paint, stapler/staples, staple removers, brads, scissors, paste, scrap materials, construction paper, paper clips, glue, glue sticks, rulers, tape • Books about favorite artists and authors as models • Computer(s) for writing and publishing • A system and materials (folders) for storing student work • Reference materials such as dictionaries, thesauruses, glossaries, language books
5. Standards-Based Center	• Guidelines for using standards-based center • Magazines, anthologies, books, and so on • Folders with graphic organizers for each standard activity • Baskets to hold folders • A system and materials (folders/container) for storing student work

(Continued)

Figure 3.7 (Continued)

Working Area	Description of Components
6. Word Study Area	• Guidelines for using word study area • Manipulative materials for developing word recognition skills • Word games, crossword puzzles (i.e., Scrabble, Jeopardy, Wheel of Fortune, Concentration) • Labeled space to house materials • A word wall area • Dry, erasable boards and pens • Magnetic boards with magnetic letters
7. Social Studies/Science Center	• Guidelines for using social studies/science center • Maps and globes • Current events board • Photographs on units of study • Informational text for units of study • Graphs and charts for units of study • Artifacts and pieces of art • Plants, class pet, and collections • Stethoscopes, thermometer, magnifying glasses, measuring devices • Journals for recording observations and experiments • Labeled space to house materials

WHAT WERE THE BIG IDEAS IN THIS CHAPTER?

Chapter 3 features suggestions that teams of teachers can examine in order to create positive, organized literacy environments. We began by describing ten needs of learners and what teachers can do to meet those needs. We also discussed types of texts that support rich literacy environments and how those texts can be organized to promote extensive reading. Considerations for grouping were outlined and various grouping options were presented that personalize reading instruction. Effective use of time and routines for managing independent and small group work were reviewed. Finally, considerations for organizing classroom space to promote literacy and a tool for student reflection and record keeping were presented.

CONSTRUCTIVE REFLECTION

Complete the following needs assessment on managing environments (Figure 3.8) for literacy to think about your team's classroom management practices and to set goals for improvement. Share your reflections with your team members.

Figure 3.8   Needs Assessment on Managing Environments for Literacy

NEEDS ASSESSMENT ON MANAGING ENVIRONMENTS FOR LITERACY			
Positive Literacy Environment	**I need help now.**	**I'm on the way.**	**I'm confident.**
My classroom is a learning community.			
My students take responsibility for their learning.			
I recognize my students' accomplishments.			
I provide authentic, relevant, and substantive tasks.			
I communicate expectations clearly.			
My students and I develop and use a code of conduct.			
My students are motivated to read and write.			
Types of Texts	**I need help now.**	**I'm on the way.**	**I'm confident.**
I have an adequate number of books per student.			
I have a wide variety of texts.			
I organize and label books for easy access.			
My classroom library includes student-generated books.			
Grouping	**I need help now.**	**I'm on the way.**	**I'm confident.**
I have varied, flexible, and dynamic groups.			
I effectively match grouping options with instructional purpose.			
I differentiate group work.			
Grouping is based on student strengths/needs.			

(Continued)

Figure 3.8   (Continued)

NEEDS ASSESSMENT ON MANAGING ENVIRONMENTS FOR LITERACY			
Use of Time	**I need help now.**	**I'm on the way.**	**I'm confident.**
I spend adequate time on Reader's Workshop.			
I spend adequate time on Writer's Workshop.			
I spend adequate time on language/ word study.			
My students read independently for adequate time.			
My students focus on comprehension for adequate time.			
Established Routines	**I need help now.**	**I'm on the way.**	**I'm confident.**
I systematically teach students routines for independent work.			
I have an effective management system for independent work.			
I review expectations for task completion at the beginning of each day.			
I implement and manage effectively multiple centers.			
Space and Recordkeeping	**I need help now.**	**I'm on the way.**	**I'm confident.**
I have an adequate area for class meetings.			
I have two small group work areas.			
There is an effective classroom library area.			
A writing/publishing center promotes writing.			
My centers promote learning of the expected reading curriculum.			
My students evaluate and keep track of tasks.			

Ensuring Student Engagement 4

Imagine this . . .

Upon walking into a third-grade classroom you are immediately struck by the fact that all students are actively engaged in reading, writing, or talking about literature. Moving around the classroom you see that some students write questions on sticky notes as they independently read different nonfiction texts about Egypt. A second group writes a reader's theater script about the annual flooding of the Nile that the group plans to perform later that week. At a kidney-shaped table, the reading specialist conducts a guided reading lesson with a group of struggling readers. In one corner of the classroom a third group of five students discusses the book *I Am the Mummy Heb-Nefert* by Eve Bunting (1997). The teacher assumes an observer role and takes notes as the students talk. Davante says, "I'm wondering how Heb-Nefert died. The book says, 'One day, disguised, my handmaiden and I went back to where I once had lived before the pharaoh's brother loved me.' Then on the next page she says, 'My parents gone now but the snake still there, still tightly coiled and sleek inside its kitchen basket. Sleepy but, I knew alert . . .' All of a sudden it seems she died. I wonder why the author didn't tell us how she died. I think the snake got her." Kiara replies, "Why do you think the snake got her?" Luiz says, "I want to piggyback on what Davante said. I infer that the snake got her because there's the picture of the snake and then nothing happens after that and Heb-Nefert says, 'I rose above myself and watched.'"

Think about your own experiences as a learner. Chances are that you learn best when the experience is meaningful to you and is relevant and you are actively engaged in applying what you learn. Exemplary literacy classrooms reflect a commitment to providing learning experiences that are similarly

48 THE LEARNING
COMMUNITIES
GUIDE TO
IMPROVING
READING
INSTRUCTION

described: The experiences provided for learners are meaningful, relevant, and engaging.

If your leadership team wants to substantially increase reading and writing proficiency, then you will want to consider what children do in exemplary classrooms. Schools and classrooms that make dramatic changes in student literacy performance allocate extensive time; use rich and varied text; foster student talk about literature; and engage students in meaningful, relevant, and substantive tasks (Allington, 2002).

WHY ARE TIME, TEXT, TALK, AND TASK IMPORTANT TO ENSURING STUDENT ENGAGEMENT?

Time. Students in exemplary classrooms engage in reading and writing for as much as half the day, as opposed to only 10% of the day in the typical classroom. The time factor is important because students need extensive time to read independently and in small groups in order to develop reading proficiency.

Text. Students need enormous quantities of successful reading in easy text, "text they [can] read accurately, fluently, and with good comprehension" (Allington, 2002, p. 743). Students who read material that matches their abilities and interests and choose much of what they read are more likely to be motivated to read. That is, success in reading nurtures reading motivation.

Talk. Past instructional approaches may not have emphasized the social aspects of learning to read and write. Students gain much insight about the process of comprehending and writing as they interact and talk with peers about literary interpretations and written responses (Pearson, Cervetti, & Jaynes, 2003). Purposeful dialogues in which students talk about ideas, strategies, and responses to books motivate readers and help them gain different perspectives. Higher level thinking and talking about text improve reading comprehension. These rich conversations are not happenstance. Students are prepared to engage in high level discussions about text much as adult book clubs guide our discussions about compelling books.

Task. Students who develop proficiency in reading and writing are engaged in active learning during most of the school day. When teachers are talking, giving directions, or providing explanations, chances are that students are not talking, reading, or writing about literature. The quality of tasks that students engage in is all important. Tasks must be substantive, challenging, meaningful, and relevant—requiring more self-regulation on the part of the reader than completing worksheets that focus on low-level, discreet, and isolated skills (Allington, 2002).

Students become self-regulated readers as they spend time engaged in reading text and applying comprehension strategies purposefully through meaningful tasks or talk. Unfortunately, in many classrooms, these types of learning opportunities are not provided consistently. This chapter focuses on the effective use of time, text, talk, and tasks to actively engage students.

WHAT CHARACTERIZES STUDENT ENGAGEMENT?

Teachers of middle grades often complain that students lack motivation to read and will not read independently. Furthermore, some teachers worry that when given the time to read, students do not understand what they read and do not know what to do about it. Reluctant readers present a real challenge and effective teachers acknowledge the link between student motivation and their instructional practices. Engagement and comprehension are synergistic because the more students are engaged, the more they comprehend and the more students comprehend, the more they are engaged in reading. Classroom practices can promote or prevent engagement. Teachers engage students when they organize content around conceptual themes and provide students with choices, interesting text, and collaborative opportunities with peers (Guthrie, 2004).

Csikszentmihalyi (1990) describes how motivation and enjoyment are linked to a state of "flow," when skill level is balanced with an appropriate level of challenge so we can maintain a deep state of focus. When readers are in flow, they are unaware of time passing, they experience pleasure from reading, and they are highly conscious of their ability to comprehend the text. Teachers encourage flow in reading when they provide opportunities for students to choose text and to talk about what they are reading with their peers. Also, students will more likely experience flow when they know that comprehending the text is doable.

WHAT INSTRUCTIONAL FRAMEWORKS PROMOTE ENGAGEMENT?

"Developing engaged readers involves helping students to become both strategic and aware of the strategies they use to read" (Baker, 2002, p. 8). When students have knowledge and control of their thinking, they become self-regulated, independent readers with a love of reading. How can teachers build motivation, independence, and engagement? Teachers can increase engagement using instructional frameworks that share certain characteristics and purposes: choice, interesting and appropriately matched text, and social interaction. Struggling readers do not become self-regulated readers without teacher intervention; therefore, initially, the teacher must provide scaffolds for engaging students productively with text.

A defining purpose of these instructional frameworks is to reduce teacher-dominated instruction so that students have choices and apply processes without prompting. The tools included in this chapter are designed to help students stay focused and concentrate on constructing meaning. These instructional frameworks include strategies students can use routinely, independently, with

50 THE LEARNING
COMMUNITIES
GUIDE TO
IMPROVING
READING
INSTRUCTION

different texts, and in different contexts. The frameworks help students apply comprehension strategies "automatically, habitually, and independently" (Block, Schaller, Joy, & Gaine, 2002, p. 43).

The next section of this book presents six instructional frameworks that promote engagement and self-regulated reading. We briefly describe the goals, steps, and procedures for each of the frameworks for increasing comprehension and provide references. We use the term *instructional frameworks* to emphasize the influential role the teacher plays in fostering active student engagement. Keep in mind that authentic student engagement occurs when students are reading, writing, and talking about text. The instructional frameworks we describe integrate several comprehension strategies that help students become more metacognitive and reflective. These frameworks also emphasize the social nature of learning to improve comprehension because they are small-group based. The frameworks include:

1. Concept-Oriented Reading Instruction

2. Reciprocal Teaching

3. Collaborative Strategic Reading

4. Say Something

5. Pivotal Point Scaffolding

6. Student-Initiated Talk After Read Aloud Lessons

Concept-Oriented Reading Instruction (CORI) (Guthrie et al., 1998)

CORI is somewhat different from the intervention tools included in this chapter. CORI is a framework for organizing reading instruction around science concepts and it may also be used with social studies concepts (Guthrie et al., 1998). The CORI framework includes four phases organized around a conceptual theme unit that takes approximately 12 weeks. The four phases are (1) observe and personalize, (2) search and retrieve, (3) comprehend and integrate, and (4) communicate to others. We chose to include CORI because it has a strong research base and integrates the teaching of reading with content and emphasizes multiple reading comprehension strategies.

The goal of CORI is to initiate and sustain reading engagement through hands-on activities, giving students choices, using interesting text, and incorporating student collaboration. CORI supports comprehension instruction with low achieving, multicultural students, as it motivates them to read and expands their sense of reading efficacy. Additionally CORI facilitates the acquisition of content knowledge.

Steps for CORI

1. Determine a conceptual theme for science or social studies, such as *animal habitats*.

2. Introduce the first phase, observe and personalize:
   (a) Engage students in observational activities related to the theme such as field trips, collecting samples, and examining specimens.
   (b) Generate questions to personalize learning based on students' interests.
   (c) Access students' prior knowledge and activate their curiosities to develop a sense of ownership for the content they will learn.

3. Initiate the second phase, search and retrieve:
   (a) Involve students in identifying books, Web sites, and other text resources related to their questions.
   (b) Teach students searching skills, such as how to use text features to locate information that responds to their questions.
   (c) Retrieve multiple books and other resources for reading and learning about the topic.

4. Conduct the third phase, comprehend and integrate:
   (a) Teach reading comprehension strategies in the context of inquiry and student-selected informational books and/or narrative materials.
   (b) Teach the comprehension skills one at a time in the first CORI unit and in the following sequence: (1) activating background knowledge, (2) questioning, (3) searching systematically for information, (4) summarizing texts, (5) monitoring comprehension during learning, (6) organizing knowledge graphically by using concept webs, and (7) communicating knowledge to others and/or organizing narratives according to plot, character, setting, and theme.
   (c) Incorporate more than one comprehension strategy when students can independently apply the strategies.

5. Implement the fourth phase, communicate to others:
   (a) Organize a culminating activity during which students share what they learned with others.
   (b) Support students in creating products such as booklets, posters, demonstrations, videos, and other product forms.
   (c) Exhibit student work.

Reciprocal Teaching (Palinscar & Brown, 1984)

Goal of Reciprocal Teaching

The goal of reciprocal teaching is to teach students explicit ways to summarize ideas, ask questions, provide clarifications, and make predictions.

Steps for Reciprocal Teaching

1. Find text that allows for clarifying, questioning, summarizing, and predicting.

2. Demonstrate the process for:
   (a) making predictions about the selection,
   (b) noticing and clarifying difficult vocabulary and concepts,
   (c) generating appropriate questions, and
   (d) summarizing the selection.

3. Form groups and have them work through a text one paragraph at a time, from four different perspectives: predictor, clarifier, questioner, and summarizer. Students may rotate roles, or a different student may take all four roles in one paragraph. The responsibilities of these roles are as follows:
   • *Predictor:* hypothesizes what will happen next
   • *Clarifier:* points out problems posed by vocabulary or text structure
   • *Questioner:* generates questions based on what has been read
   • *Summarizer:* Gives a brief summary

4. Provide guidance and feedback to students.

Collaborative Strategic Reading (CSR) (Klingner & Vaughn, 1998)

The goal of CSR is to teach students explicit ways to (1) activate prior knowledge, (2) predict, (3) click and clunk or monitor comprehension during reading by identifying difficult words and concepts and using fix-up strategies when the text does not make sense, (4) identify the gist, and (5) summarize. CSR also builds word recognition strategies.

Steps for CSR

1. Provide direct explanation and modeling with the full class.
2. Place students into small, collaborative groups and assign roles, such as:
   (a) Prediction expert
   (b) Clunk expert
   (c) Gist expert
   (d) Announcer, who decides who reads next
   (e) Encourager

3. Preview before reading:
   (a) Brainstorm: What do we already know about the topic?
   (b) Predict using these guidelines: (1) What do we think we will learn about the topic when we read the passages? (2) Find the clues in the title, headings, pictures, and key words.

4. Clink and clunk during reading:
   (a) Monitor: Were there any parts of words that were hard to understand (clunks)?
   (b) Fix-up: How can we fix the clunks? Provide cue cards of the following:
      • Reread the sentence and look for key ideas.
      • Reread the sentence leaving out the clunk. What word makes sense?
      • Reread the sentence before and after the clunk looking for clues.
      • Look for a prefix or a suffix in the word.
      • Break the word apart and look for smaller words.

5. Get the gist during reading:
   (a) Ask questions:
      • What is the most important person, place, or thing?
      • What is the most important idea about the person, place, or thing?
   (b) Paraphrase: Answer the above questions in ten words or less.

6. Wrap up after reading:
   (a) Ask questions:
      • What questions would help us check to see whether we understand the most important information in the passage?
      • Can we answer the questions?
   (b) Review: What did we learn?

SOURCE: J. K. Klingner and Sharon Vaughn (1998). "Using Collaborative Strategic Reading." *Teaching Exceptional Children*, July/August 1998. Copyright 1998 CEC. Reprinted with permission.

Say Something (Beers, 2003; Harste, Shorte, & Burke, 1996)

The goal of Say Something is to teach students explicit ways to make predictions, ask questions, clarify, make comments, and make connections.

Steps for Say Something

1. Find an appropriate text.

2. Establish small groups of two to three students who will take turns reading out loud three to four paragraphs of the text.

3. Explain the procedure by going over the rules:
   (a) With your partner decide who will say something first.
   (b) When you say something:
      • Make a prediction
      • Ask a question
      • Clarify something you had misunderstood
      • Make a comment
      • Make a connection
   (c) If you cannot do one of the five things, then reread.

4. Model the strategy with a partner or put the dialogue on a transparency.

5. Explain that the partner's responsibility is to respond to what the person said.

6. Have students use this intervention tool with short passages.

7. Observe and provide scaffolding and feedback.

8. Model the strategy often.

9. Provide posters with stem starters for each of the five areas.

Pivotal Point Scaffolding (Block et al., 2002)

The goal of Pivotal Point Scaffolding is to scaffold students' monitoring during reading of difficult text, promote engagement during sustained silent reading, and assess student use of comprehension strategies. *Steps for Pivotal Point Scaffolding:*

1. Allocate a developmentally appropriate number of minutes for sustained silent reading.

2. Assist readers one-on-one during the independent reading time when they have problems.

3. Use the PAR technique to form feedback statements for students: praise, ask, raise:
   • *Praise* students for using a particular comprehension process.
   • *Ask* individuals how they knew to use that process and what help they need with comprehension.
   • *Raise* students' ability by demonstrating the next higher type of support and processes that address what the student needs.

4. Record the difficulty that stumped a student's ability to make meaning on a pivotal record form.

5. Use this data to organize groups for comprehension mini-lessons.

> ***Student-Initiated Talk After Read Aloud Lessons (STAR)*** (Block et al., 2002)
>
> The goal of Student-Initiated Talk After Read Aloud Lessons is to teach students explicit ways to make connections.
>
> *Steps for STAR*
>
> 1. Read aloud a text.
>
> 2. Use books that:
>   (a) Contain a surprise that reversed the plot
>   (b) Include action-filled segments
>   (c) Portray characters whom students could easily relate to and who repeatedly attempted to resolve problems and said or did insightful things
>   (d) Feature events that triggered a change in the usual order of events that occur in students' lives
>
> 3. Pause during read aloud if students want to talk about what the section means or if they have questions and allow students to have greater control over the dialogue.
>
> 4. Maintain records of students who think aloud and what they think aloud about.

WHAT CAN WE DO TO PROMOTE HIGHER LEVEL THINKING AND TALK ABOUT TEXT?

"It is more critical for dependent readers to talk about texts during the reading experience than after it" (Beers, 2003, p. 104). Dependent readers need support while reading text to engage in higher level thinking and talking about text. What is higher level talk about text? Traditionally, teachers asked a battery of questions, recitation style, at the end of a reading selection. Often, this approach does not support higher level thinking, comprehension, or student engagement. It is talk about text that, "invites students to make connections between a given text and their experiences, the world, the author, and one part of a text and another" (Pearson et al., 2003). Higher order talk about text emphasizes five *comprehension moves* that students are encouraged to use when talking about text: (1) making connections, (2) making predictions, (3) asking questions or wondering, (4) recalling, and (5) inferring. Figure 4.1 provides an overview of comprehension moves or strategies, definitions for the moves, and sample conversational stem statements. This table provides teachers and students with a resource for initiating and nurturing high-level thinking in conversations about text.

These comprehension moves often differ from what typically occurs in classrooms when teachers question students in a recitation style. We know from our work involving observations of hundreds of classrooms that novice teachers are more likely to use lower level questioning than higher level

Figure 4.1   Comprehension Moves for Promoting Higher Level Talk About Text

Comprehension Move	Definition	Example
Making connections	Connecting the text to personal experience	That part reminded me of when my brother . . .
	Connecting the parts of the text to earlier parts of the text	It's kind of like that part in the beginning when the teacher says . . .
	Connecting the text to other texts	That's like that other book we read where the main character . . .
	Connecting the text to the world	This sounds like that thing that happened in San Diego . . .
	Connecting the text to the writer	It seems like the author wants us to learn something about how friends sometimes . . .
Making predictions	Using evidence from personal experience, prior knowledge, or the text to make good guesses about what's coming next, how a problem might be solved, and so on	I predict that . . . I'm guessing that . . . He's probably going to . . .
Asking questions or wondering	Posing questions about the text, the characters, the author, and so on	I wonder why she . . . How do you think the father felt when he . . . Why did the author put in that part about the . . .
Recalling	Paraphrasing or summarizing the text	Well, first the main character went to the playground, but then she . . .
Inferring	Integrating prior knowledge with new information in an effort to construct coherent meaning	You can tell she was worried because . . .

SOURCE: Pearson et al. (2003)

questioning, resulting in superficial talk about text. Moreover, we have observed that questioning is used primarily to assess rather than to instruct or to engage students in meaningful conversations about text. The quality of the teacher's questions influences the quality of student responses, and teachers may need concrete examples and support in order to use questioning that stimulates rich student talk about literature.

56 THE LEARNING
COMMUNITIES
GUIDE TO
IMPROVING
READING
INSTRUCTION

To initiate instruction on conversation and comprehension moves, first introduce conversational norms that support higher level talk about text. Establishing norms creates a climate for honoring diversity and set expectations for how group members behave during discussions. Pearson and others (Pearson et al., 2003) recommend norms for dialogue that include the following:

- Talk and listen to each other, not just to the teacher, and avoid interrupting the speaker or talking the same time as others.

- Avoid monopolizing the conversation.

- Connect comments to or "piggyback on" a previous speaker's comments.

- Announce when you intend to change the topic, but do not jump from one topic to another too quickly.

- Decide how to take turns talking and follow the agreed upon procedures.

- Back up your opinions or be open about your uncertainties.

- Respect different opinions but feel free to disagree.

After presenting conversation norms, teach students how to use conversational moves in dialogue about books. Teach these moves explicitly by modeling and scaffolding during real conversations about text. Define and teach conversational moves and provide students with samples of what they can say to use a particular move. Figure 4.2 defines twelve conversational moves and gives an example of student talk for each move. Additionally, the figure includes suggestions for what teachers can say to scaffold student use of the conversational move (Pearson et al., 2003).

Figure 4.2   Overview of Conversational Moves

Conversational Move	Definition	Student Talk Example	Teacher Talk Scaffold
Restating	Repeating a previous contribution	Linda said that the fish was sad because he was lonely.	Can someone say that in a different way?
Inviting	Inviting a participant to contribute	I'd like to hear what George thinks.	Do you want to invite anyone else to add to what you said?
Acknowledging or validating	Recognizing a response without agreeing or disagreeing	I can see why you said that. I get what you're saying. I hadn't thought of that.	Do you get what Juan is trying to say here?

Conversational Move	Definition	Student Talk Example	Teacher Talk Scaffold
Focusing or refocusing	Making a meta-comment about the course of the conversation	We were talking about the reasons that Frank ran away from home.	I think I've lost track of the question we were trying to answer. Can anyone help me here?
Agreeing		I agree because . . . Yeah . . . That's right because . . .	Does anyone agree with Juan?
Disagreeing		I see what you're saying, but . . . But what about . . . ? I disagree, because . . .	Does anyone want to disagree? Does anyone see it another way?
Elaborating	Extending one's own or another's assertion	I agree with Juan that the fish was lonely, and I think that he . . . Also . . .	Does anyone want to say something more about that? Who can think of another solution or another reason?
Requesting clarification		What do you mean? Can you say more about that? What makes you think that?	Does anyone find anything confusing in this part of the story?
Providing an example	Providing an example from inside the text or outside to support one's own or another's assertion.	For example . . . It's like when . . .	Can you give examples of . . . from the story? Has anything like this ever happened to you or someone you know?
Signaling a change	Changing the direction of the conversation	I want to talk about the mother.	Does anyone want to change the subject? Are you ready to move on?
Providing evidence	Supporting one's own or another's assertions with evidence	I agree with Julie that the fish was sad. You can see his sad face in the picture on page 3.	Why do you think that? Is there anything in the story to support that idea?
Posing a question to the group		Does anyone think . . . ?	Do you have a question for the group?

SOURCE: Pearson et al. (2003)

When combined, the use of conversational norms and moves can result in high student engagement and higher level thinking. This type of engagement reflects best practices in literacy instruction because it nurtures student comprehension through social interactions, application of multiple comprehension strategies, and immersion in literature discussion that is both purposeful and motivating. Students' motivation is heightened because of the ownership and autonomy they experience through dialogue. The procedure for planning and scaffolding higher level questions and higher level talk about text (HOQ and HLTT) is summarized below.

Higher Order Questions and Talk About Text (HOQ and HLTT)
(Pearson et al., 2003)

The goal of Higher Order Questions and Talk About Text is to scaffold students' higher level talk about text and promote active engagement in book discussions

Steps for Higher Order Questions and Talk About Text:

1. Choose a text that will lead to rich discussion and read to identify what ideas, connections, and questions come to mind.

2. Select a comprehension move that matches your list of ideas, connections, and questions from the text.

3. Identify a conversation norm to teach that fits well with the identified comprehension move.

4. Review any previously taught conversation and comprehension moves.

5. Introduce the conversation norms and comprehension moves for the lesson.

6. Model with a think aloud and create the following chart of comprehension and conversation moves.

    What Good Readers Do

    How We Talk About Text

7. Invite students to begin the discussion or start with an open-ended question such as, What is the big idea of this book? Or So what do you think?

8. Encourage students to use the list of conversational moves during discussion.

9. Take notes on student use of comprehension and conversation moves and share with students on the chart.

Using the higher-level questions and talk about text strategies, teachers can teach students how to actively participate in stimulating conversations about texts and increase student engagement in reading. The beauty of promoting higher-level questioning and talking about text is that it can be applied flexibly to teachers' existing instructional models and materials. For instance, teachers can use these strategies with trade books or basals. Video tapes of students using comprehension and conversational moves are helpful in showing what these conversations can sound like and look like. Moreover, this approach is realistic and respectful of teachers' time, as it requires limited planning time.

HOW CAN WE ENGAGE STUDENTS IN WRITING AND THINKING ABOUT THEIR READING?

Teachers can help students write about their reading in ways similar to those teachers use to help students talk about their reading.

> When we write—we put our thinking onto the page—so we can hold onto our fleeting thoughts. When we write, we can hold our thoughts in our hand, we can put our thoughts in our pocket, and we can bring out yesterday's thoughts. (Calkins, 2001, p. 372)

When students write and share their writing with others, they improve their thinking. Students improve their thinking by asking such questions as, What's the big idea? What patterns do I see? How are our ideas alike?

The following section presents six intervention tools for engaging students in writing and thinking about the books and other texts they read. The presentation of intervention tools for writing in response to reading follows the same format as the comprehension strategy tools. The writing intervention tools include the following:

- Read It, Think It, Post It, Write It

- Writer's Inquiry

- Concept-Based Analysis of Story Elements

- Identifying What Is Most Important

- Readers' Theater

- Double-Entry Journals

Read It, Think It, Post It, Write It

The goals of Read It, Think It, Post It, Write It are to make students' thinking about reading evident and to help students to be more metacognitive about their reading and writing.

Steps for Read It, Think It, Post It, Write It

1. Identify a comprehension strategy, story element, or literary skill such as author style.

2. Ask students to apply the targeted strategy with a self-selected text.

3. Group students individually, in pairs, or in small groups.

4. Instruct students to focus on the targeted strategy as they pause while reading to write their responses on sticky notes. Students place sticky notes on the page of the text where they used the strategy.

5. Provide time for pairs or small groups to get together to review and talk about their book, using their sticky notes.

6. Ask students to use blank paper to organize their sticky notes, picking and choosing a few sticky notes to use in writing about the text.

7. Provide time for students to write either individually or collaboratively about their text.

Writer's Inquiry (Ray, 1999)

The goals of Writer's Inquiry are to provide an opportunity for students to apply the schema comprehension strategy and to engage students in using literature as a model for writing.

Steps for Writer's Inquiry

1. Identify a text to read aloud. Pause from time to time and ask students to notice something about the craft of the text.

2. Ask the students to talk about the text and generate a theory about why the author used that craft; give the technique a name.

3. Ask students to identify other texts in which authors used the same craft. Post a list of these authors and their texts.

4. Collect texts that reflect the writer's craft discussed, texts the students identified during the discussion, or self-selected texts.

5. Allow students to work in pairs or in small groups to analyze the text in terms of identified craft. Use the following graphic organizer to guide analysis. Complete the first column during a whole-group think-aloud discussion. The teacher may identify the techniques the students use in their analysis.

Technique	Purpose of Technique	Author	Example of Author's Use	Example in Our Writing

6. Conduct conferences with pairs or groups to discuss techniques and student samples of writing using the technique.

7. Expand students' abilities to analyze text so that students self-select an author, look at several texts the author has written, and identify writing techniques.

8. Repeat writer's inquiry using identified techniques or identify techniques in their own writing.

Concept-Based Analysis of Story Elements

The goal of Concept-Based Analysis of Story Elements is to make connections from text-to-text and text-to-self using the concept of change.

Steps for Concept-Based Analysis of Story Elements

1. Identify several texts that can be analyzed through the concept of change.

2. Conduct a read aloud of one of the texts.

3. Introduce the change matrix featured below, using an overhead transparency.

Title and Author	Changes in Characters	Changes in Setting	Changes in Relationships	Changes in You as the Result of Reading

4. Reread the story and model a think aloud using the change matrix.

5. Model responses for each of the column headings using complete sentences.

6. Identify several pieces of literature for students to read that relate to the concept of change.

7. Ask students to complete the change matrix individually, in pairs, or in small groups. Students use complete sentences to respond to each of the column headings.

8. Conference with individuals, pairs, or small groups about the connections they made to the concept of change.

9. Ask students to identify other books in which the characters, setting, and relationships change.

10. Ask students to write about how reading a particular piece of literature changed their lives.

SOURCE: Center for Gifted Education (1998)

Identifying What Is Most Important

The goals of Identifying What Is Most Important are to help students identify the most important facts and to use literature as a model for writing and comprehending.

- To link reading, thinking, and writing.
- To help students to be more metacognitive about their reading and writing.

Steps for Identifying What Is Most Important

1. Use the text *The Important Book* by Margaret Wise Brown (1949).

2. Explain that one strategy good readers use is identifying what is most important in a text.

3. Prepare students for a read aloud of *The Important Book.* Tell students to think about how the author writes the text and to determine the author's rationale for identifying what is most important about each object.

4. Ask students to predict the things they expect that the author included in the book.

5. Read aloud the first page of *The Important Book* and ask students for other possible responses or descriptive phrases.

6. Continue to read the book for two to three more pages.

7. Ask students about what they notice about how the author writes each of the pages to identify writing style and note that each page
   (a) Begins with "The important thing about a . . . is . . ."
   (b) four or five facts about the item introduced in the opening sentence
   (c) Repeats the first sentence as the last line

8. Continue to read the remainder of the text, pausing before reading a page to have students predict what the author will say is most important about an item.

9. Brainstorm things that are important to students and ask them to create a page for a class *Important Book.*

10. Instruct each student to use a blank sheet of paper to prepare a page for the class Important Book by applying the techniques that Margaret Wise Brown used to write her book. Ask students to illustrate their book pages.

11. Ask students to describe their thinking about what is important about their item for the book.

12. Confer with students as they prepare a page of the book.

13. Bind the book and read it aloud to the class.

14. Culminate the session by having students respond to the following prompt in their journals: "I learned that when it comes to identifying what is most important for text . . ."

64 THE LEARNING
COMMUNITIES
GUIDE TO
IMPROVING
READING
INSTRUCTION

Readers' Theater (Robb, 2000a; Fountas & Pinnell, 2001)

The goals of Readers' Theater are to reread a text to increase fluency, to read text critically to interpret what parts to rewrite into a readers' theater script, and to integrate reading and writing by creating a script of the important information or favorite parts of the text.

Steps for Readers' Theater

1. Identify a text, narrative, or informational to turn into a play.

2. Provide a sample script and describe what a readers' theater script looks like. Tell students to include a narrator and the characters in their selected chapter or passage.

3. Help students find a text passage that contains rich dialogue and a problem or conflict.

4. Model how to write dialogue from text taking the exact words characters say and writing them into parts. Add feelings or suggestions for how the character will express the parts in parentheses beside the parts. For example: Peter: "I really am too sick to go to school" (coughing and whining).

5. Show students how to take information from the passage to create background descriptions of plot, setting, and events for the parts of the narrator(s).

6. Gather any essential props.

7. Decide who plays what part and provide time for practice reading.

8. Perform the readers' theater for an audience and allow students to use the script. Students do not memorize the script.

Double-Entry Journals (Beers, 2003; Robb, 2000a)

The goals of double-entry journals are to provide a structure for responding to text and for taking notes, to support student monitoring of comprehension during reading, and to support student use of multiple comprehension strategies to construct meaning (i.e., predicting, making connections, summarizing, determining the important ideas). Additionally, these journals inform the teacher about students' comprehension and their use of strategies.

Steps for Double-Entry Journals

1. Ask students to draw a line down the middle of their notebook or fold a piece of paper in half to create two columns.

2. Model how to set up a journal page and demonstrate how to respond to the prompts.

   What Is in the Book

   Notes From My Mind

3. Instruct students to record a word or phrase from the text in the left column and include the page number.

4. Ask students to record their comments in the right column, which could include questions, connections they made, or graphic symbols.

5. Vary by asking students to use abbreviations to note the type of comprehension strategy used for challenging text. For example, TS for text-to-self connections, TT for text-to-text connections, TW for text-to-world, P for predicting.

6. Consider another variation for double-entry journals and have students select a quote. Students copy the one- to three-sentence quote in the left column and then in the right column, respond to one or more of the following:
   (a) Explain why this quote struck you and how it made you feel.
   (b) Connect this quote to your life or to another book.
   (c) Connect the quote to a character, event, or theme.

66 THE LEARNING
COMMUNITIES
GUIDE TO
IMPROVING
READING
INSTRUCTION

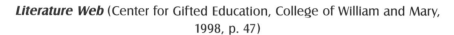

Literature Web (Center for Gifted Education, College of William and Mary,
1998, p. 47)

The goals of the Literature Web are to provide a structure for analyzing and
interpreting text and to promote higher level thinking and talking about text. In
particular, the Literature Web highlights those aspects of literature upon which
inferences are derived, such as figurative language, feelings, structure of text,
and vocabulary.

Steps for the Literature Web

Before Reading:

- Present and explain the graphic organizer "Literature Web" to the whole
  class, using an overhead projector and transparency. (See facing page.)
- Ask the students if they have ever seen wild geese flying and describe
  what they saw.
- Select and present a poem by using a transparency and handout and
  having one student read the poem to the entire class.
- Instruct the class that they will be asked to read the poem and use the
  graphic organizer individually to interpret the poem and that the poem will
  be reexamined in small group and whole group.

During Reading:

- Allow 15 minutes for the students to read the poem on their own and
  complete the graphic organizer on their own.
- Circulate through the room and assist students who seem to be having
  difficulty in completing the assignment. Ask questions to elicit
  understanding and determine the connections students are making.
- Take notes about individual students' responses to the assignment, noting
  in particular those who seem to be having difficulty with certain aspects
  of the web.

After Reading:

- Place the students in cooperative groups of four.
- Identify a materials manager, reporter, recorder, and encourager/time
  keeper.
- Instruct the students to recreate the literature web on chart paper. Explain
  that for each of the components of the web, each student should tell
  the recorder what was written for each part of the web in the following
  order: (1) key words, (2) feelings, (3) images/symbols, (4) structure, and
  (5) ideas.
- Instruct the students to discuss why they included what they did for each
  of the components.
- Provide 25 minutes for the groups to complete the task and circulate as
  they are working.
- Process small group findings in a large group setting.
- Ask each student to write one summary statement about the main theme
  of the poem.

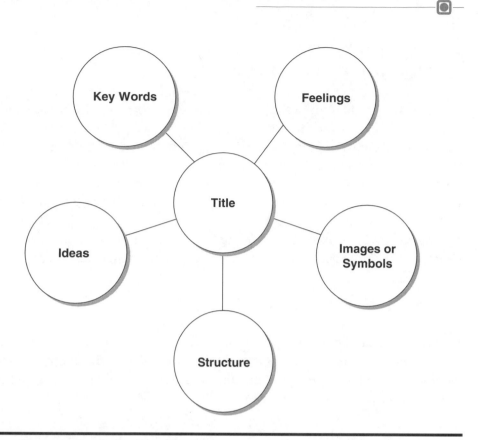

SOURCE: Center for Gifted Education (1999)

Exemplary classrooms are those in which students are highly engaged in reading, writing, and talking about text. However, if students are engaged in simplistic tasks that do not ask much of them as thinkers, it is not likely that the learning experiences will yield better readers, thinkers, and writers. In other words, all engagement is not equal. Rather, the type of student engagement that leads to improved reading and writing "is not an automatic by-product of learning to recognize words or learning to write but depends on immersion in *interesting* reading and writing and learning experiences" (Pressley, 2002, p. 86). The intervention tools for reading, talking about text, and writing in response to text reflect the best practices in student engagement and share the following characteristics:

- Support students in becoming independent readers

- Incorporate multiple comprehension strategies

- Integrate multiple ways of learning

- Encourage teachers to provide students with choice

- Use rich text as the foundation for learning and applying strategies

- Require students to think about themselves as learners

- Require students to actively respond to literature

68 THE LEARNING
COMMUNITIES
GUIDE TO
IMPROVING
READING
INSTRUCTION

WHAT WERE THE BIG IDEAS IN THIS CHAPTER?

This chapter provides an overview of strategies to engage students in reading, writing, and talking about text at high levels. We began by describing the role that time, text, talk, and tasks play in actively engaging students and discussed the link between metacognition and engagement. Next, instructional frameworks that promote metacognitive, self-regulated readers were presented. Also discussed were strategies that can be used to promote higher level thinking and talk about text. Finally, we introduced instructional frameworks for engaging students in writing and thinking about their reading. The ideas and strategies featured in this chapter will help instructional teams promote student engagement across classes.

CONSTRUCTIVE REFLECTION

Review the thirteen instructional frameworks that were described in this chapter with your instructional team. ACE a summary of the chapter by completing the graphic organizer to identify *a*dvantages, *c*oncerns, and *e*nlightening thoughts for each tool (Figure 4.3).

Figure 4.3   Summary of Chapter 4 Instructional Frameworks

Instructional Framework	Advantages	Concerns	Enlightening
1. Reciprocal Teaching			
2. Collaborative Strategic Reading (CSR)			
3. Say Something			
4. Student-Initiated Talk After Read Aloud (STAR)			
5. Pivotal Point Scaffolding			

Instructional Framework	Advantages	Concerns	Enlightening
6. Concept-Oriented Reading Instruction (CORI)			
7. Higher Order Questions & Higher Order Talk About Text			
8. Read, It, Think It, Post It, Write It			
9. Writer's Inquiry			
10. Concept-Based Analysis of Story Elements			
11. Identifying What Is Most Important			
12. Readers' Theater			
13. Double-Entry Journals			

Emphasizing Active Teaching 5

Imagine this . . .

A first-year teacher has found that many of her students do not comprehend as well as they should. For three weeks the young teacher has given her students reading passages and asked them to identify the most important ideas—but many still don't seem to get it. Frustrated, the teacher seeks the help of her mentor teacher and relates all that her students have done to learn how to identify the most important facts in fiction and nonfiction texts. The mentor teacher actively listens to the third-grade teacher's woes and asks one key question: "Have you modeled what you do as a reader to identify the most important points in a text?" The teacher replies, "Yes—I explain the most important ideas." The mentor teacher responds by saying, "I hear you say that you 'explain,' but do you model?" With a quizzical look on her face, the first-year teacher asks, "What do you mean?"

As teachers, we are responsible for what our students learn and know; we make the difference in what they learn and how they learn. We work hard planning and delivering instruction, and sometimes our students do not achieve the desired results. Intuitively, we know that not all instructional strategies are equal, but which strategies and practices will help us to accomplish what we so diligently strive to achieve—increased student engagement and achievement? How can we plan for effective teacher engagement? By focusing on creating a climate for learning and selectively using certain instructional practices and models, we can provide instruction that will lead to learning.

WHAT CHARACTERIZES EXEMPLARY CLASSROOMS?

Recent research informs us about what accomplished teachers do to shape successful learning for literacy (Taylor, Pressley, & Pearson, 2002). When

72 THE LEARNING
COMMUNITIES
GUIDE TO
IMPROVING
READING
INSTRUCTION

researchers observed accomplished teachers who beat the odds to improve student reading performance, they found several common characteristics across classrooms. Specifically, accomplished teachers:

- Provide time for independent reading

- Maintain high levels of student engagement

- Emphasize small group instruction

- Supplement explicit phonics instruction with coaching students in applying phonics to real texts

- Emphasize all levels of comprehension and writing in response to reading

- Reach out to parents as partners

Allington's study of effective teachers over a decade provides additional insights to inform classroom practice. Allington found that "effective teachers manage to produce better achievement regardless of which curricular materials, pedagogical approach, or reading program they use" (Allington, 2002, p. 742). Allington, identified six Ts in high performing classrooms: time, tasks, texts, teaching, talk, and testing (Figure 5.1).

Research on the brain and learning also has implications for creating high performing reading classrooms that nurture Allington's six Ts. We know

Figure 5.1   Six T's of Exemplary Reading Instruction

What Do Exemplary Reading Teachers Do?	
Time	Allocate as much as half of the school day for actual reading and writing.
Tasks	Assign substantive and challenging tasks that engage students over multiple school days rather than multiple worksheets.
Texts	Provide a wealth of fiction and nonfiction books, in a wide range of reading levels, so that all children can perform at high levels of accuracy, fluency, and comprehension.
Teaching	Rely on active teaching (e.g., modeling, demonstrating, explicit explanations, thinking aloud to demonstrate what good readers do when they read).
Talk	Invite conversations about books that stimulate deeper thinking, are not teacher-directed, and decrease "interrogation" with many recall questions at the end of a page or story.
Testing	Evaluate student work based on effort and improvement using rubric schemes.

SOURCE: Allington (2002)

teachers can create certain conditions for learning that reflect what is known about how students learn best. Fogarty (2002) integrated research on the brain and learning into a "four-corner framework" for brain compatible classrooms. Based upon the research of Caine and Caine, Sylwester, Goldman and others, the four corner framework of brain compatible classrooms provides a balanced overview of considerations for effective teacher engagement. In general, we learn best in classrooms where teachers (1) create a climate for learning, (2) teach skills explicitly and methodically, (3) provide authentic opportunities for students to apply and interact with content, and (4) nurture reflection and self-assessment. How can we apply this framework specifically to classrooms that encourage literacy? Figure 5.2 presents a self-assessment to support teachers in designing nonthreatening classrooms that nurture thinking, reading, and writing.

Figure 5.2   Self-Assessment for Thoughtful and Literate Classrooms

Do I Create a Climate Conducive to Developing Literacy?	Yes (+) No (−) Not Sure (?)
Provide reading materials and instruction that will appropriately challenge students—not too difficult or easy.	
Create an enriched environment with classroom libraries that include fiction and nonfiction reading materials in varying genres, topics, and themes.	
Reduce threat by getting to know students' strengths, weaknesses, and interests as readers.	
Foster emotional involvement in reading using varied instructional techniques such as accessing students' prior knowledge and experience.	
Create flexible groups based on students' interests, skill needs, strengths, and reading materials.	
Do I Explicitly Teach the Skills Necessary for Reading and Writing?	Yes (+) No (−) Not Sure (?)
Apply a gradual release of responsibility when teaching students to read and write.	
Identify explicit reading skills based on students' strengths and needs.	
Provide learning experiences that focus on vocabulary, phonics, phonemic awareness, comprehension, and fluency.	
Use modeling to demonstrate the thinking processes necessary for reading.	
Provide scaffolding and coaching when students are applying reading strategies.	
Identify reading strategies to be taught and allow students to apply strategies using varied, appropriately leveled text.	
Incorporate cooperative learning, literature circles, paired reading, and other interactive groupings.	
Use graphic organizers to guide students' reading.	

(Continued)

74 THE LEARNING
COMMUNITIES
GUIDE TO
IMPROVING
READING
INSTRUCTION

Figure 5.2 (Continued)

Do I Provide Authentic Interactions With Reading and Writing?	Yes (+) No (–) Not Sure (?)
Use effective high-level questions to guide students' thinking before, during, and after reading and writing.	
Apply active learning techniques that engage students in using manipulatives and technology to read and write.	
Embed the teaching of reading skills within the reading of rich fiction and nonfiction literature.	
Employ varied instructional techniques that honor students' varied learning styles, multiple intelligences, and ways of learning.	
Encourage students to read for specific, authentic purposes.	
Do I Nurture Reflection and Self-Assessment in Reading and Writing?	Yes (+) No (–) Not Sure (?)
Provide students with varied opportunities to reflect on what they are reading and writing and how they are reading and writing.	
Provide reflection prompts to guide students' interactions with reading and writing.	
Use varied assessment strategies, such as portfolios, performance assessments, and running records, to determine students' strengths, weaknesses, and acquisition of skills.	
Guide students' self-evaluation through use of rubrics that provide specific and clear criteria for effective reading and writing.	

HOW CAN WE INCREASE LEARNER-SCAFFOLDED VERSUS TEACHER-CONTROLLED INSTRUCTION?

In essence, nonthreatening classrooms that nurture thinking, reading, and writing are defined by teacher interactions that are learner directed and focus on providing varied levels of support in the learning process. A fundamental belief of accomplished teachers is that all students can succeed in reading, if provided with appropriate levels of instructional support. Considering how we teach is just as important as what we teach (Pressley, 2003). Accomplished teachers use a student support stance more frequently than a teacher-direct stance (Taylor et al., 2002). While a student-support stance is desired practice, this stance may not be widely practiced in reading instruction. Taylor and Pearson (2000) found that less than 10% of upper elementary teachers used a student-support interaction of modeling, and 75% of the least accomplished teachers preferred telling students information. Also, our own observations of over 200 elementary classrooms in Virginia found predominately teacher-controlled instruction that typically promoted passive student engagement.

What should teachers do to increase student-support interactions and decrease teacher-controlled interactions? The Russian psychologist, Lev Vygotsky (1978), maintained that what a learner does initially with assistance, he or she can do independently in the future. Vygotsky coined the term *zone of proximal development* to advocate that every learner, no matter what the task, needs initial modeling, concrete support of an expert in order to master the task and do it independently. As teachers, we apply this concept when we work through the teaching-learning zone in reading instruction (Routman, 2003; Fountas & Pinnell, 2001).

For example, when teachers are introducing visualization as a comprehension strategy, they model how they visualize by thinking aloud while reading poems or short passages. They make their thinking evident to their students by describing what they see in their mind's eyes while reading. Next, they ask their students to turn to one another and describe what they see when a short passage is read. They continue this kind of *guided practice* until they think the students are ready to apply the practice independently. During *independent practice*, students read self-selected, appropriately leveled text and record their visualizations on sticky notes. Teachers circulate and review the students' notes and provide scaffolding or coach students who are struggling with visualization or not using it appropriately. After independent practice, teachers pull the groups together again and engage their students in *reflection* by asking them to describe examples of their visualizations and the pluses and minuses of using visualization to comprehend. After repeated *application* of visualization in different contexts and texts, the students become more independent and skilled in use of the strategy.

The teaching-learning zone (Figure 5.3) suggests that teachers consciously use modeling and coaching for instruction as prevalent teaching techniques. Modeling and coaching used consistently make a difference in student reading performance. For example, exemplary teachers begin by explaining or demystifying the thinking processes needed to comprehend text (Duffy, 2003). Explanations, within authentic text, and modeling provide students a concrete, verbal demonstration of strategies good readers use to construct meaning. Student-scaffolded teaching enhances students' ability to apply reading strategies and increases student achievement. Figure 5.4 provides an overview of teacher-controlled and student-scaffolded practices (Allington & Johnson, 2002; Taylor et al., 2002).

What do teacher-controlled and student-scaffolded behaviors look like and sound like? By understanding the differences between these two styles and the impact they make on learning, teachers and instructional teams can more thoughtfully guide professional growth to increase reading achievement. Figure 5.5 lists the behaviors and describes what the two styles look like and sound like. Instructional teams might use this list to think about and discuss the interaction stances they most frequently use.

Figure 5.3   The Teaching-Learning Zone

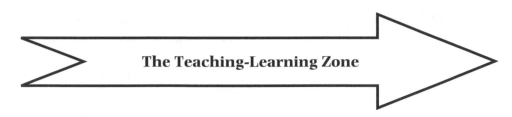

Modeling Teacher	Guided Practice Teacher	Independent Practice Teacher	Reflection Teacher	Application Teacher
• Demonstrates how to apply • Models • Thinks aloud • Explains	• Practices with students • Observes • Validates • Supports • Coaches • Scaffolds • Gives feedback • Re-teaches • Clarifies	• Responds • Assesses • Observes/ listens • Gives feedback • Sets goals • Assists when needed	• Prompts • Encourages • Questions • Invites	• Encourages • Observes • Assesses
				Student • Applies strategy to new genre, context, or format • Demonstrates effective use of strategy • Becomes a more self-regulated reader and writer
			Student • Self-assesses • Thinks about what he or she did well or could do differently • Thinks about how to apply strategy in different genres, contexts, and so on • Determines how strategy aids in reading or writing	
		Student • Applies on own • Self-directs • Confirms • Self-evaluates • Monitors • Receives feedback		
	Student • Applies • Practices with teacher • Problem solves • Shares thinking			
Student • Listens • Observes				

Figure 5.4   Interaction Stances

Teacher Controlled Interactions
• Tell or give information.
• Engage students in recitation or a series of questions that do not require deep thinking.

Student Scaffolded Interactions
• Explain thinking processes for reading.
• Model or demonstrate how to do something
• Coach or scaffold
• Listen and provide feedback

◉ Figure 5.5   Teacher-Controlled Behaviors Versus Student-Scaffolded Behaviors

Teacher-Controlled Behaviors	Student-Scaffolded Behaviors
Telling Students Information . . . Looks Like? Sounds Like?	*Modeling or Demonstrating . . . Looks Like? Sounds Like?*
• *Looks like* teacher giving facts in abstract format without directions or how to use the information. • *Sounds like* "The main idea is what a passage is primarily about. Find the main idea of this passage."	• *Looks like* teacher showing strategies that effective learners use to acquire and apply knowledge. When modeling, teachers (1) explain the strategy, (2) demonstrate how to apply the strategy, and (3) think aloud to show the mental processes used. • *Sounds like* after reading a passage in a text, the teacher stops and says, "I'm wondering what the most important point of this passage is. I see that one sentence in this paragraph says that Lola looked for her sister in the park. Another says she went to her sister's friend's house. A third says Lola went to the school to find her sister. She looked for her sister in many places. I think the central idea of this paragraph is that Lola looked for her sister in many places."
Recitation . . . *Looks Like? Sounds Like?*	*Coaching and Scaffolding . . .* *Looks Like? Sounds Like?*
• *Looks like* teacher asking individual students, in a whole group setting, a series of questions to which they respond so that the interactions are question, answer, question, answer, so on. • *Sounds like* "What is the main idea, Latesha? Who is the main character, Sue? What did he do, Jose? When did the story take place, Leo?"	• *Looks like* teacher supports, prompts, questions, coaches, or uses a graphic organizer as student tries to perform a task. • *Sounds like* "I can see that you are having difficulty identifying the central idea of this passage, Liah. Tell me what you're thinking about (listens to student). Sometimes it helps to identify what we think are important sentences, for they might lead to the central idea. Pick a sentence you think is important and read it to me. What makes you think this is an important sentence? Are there any other sentences that you think are important? Why? Looking at these sentences, what do you think might be the central idea of this passage?"
Explain How to Do Something . . . *Looks Like? Sounds Like?*	*Listen and Provide Feedback . . .* *Looks Like? Sounds Like?*
• *Looks like* giving step-by-step instructions verbally without a demonstration. • *Sounds like* "To write a good paragraph, you need to have a topic sentence. Then write about three sentences that say something about the topic sentence. Now, I'd like you to write a paragraph describing your favorite pastime."	• *Looks like* teacher observing individuals performing a task, listening to individual responses, and giving specific instructional feedback or suggestions to improve work, to support student, or to affirm mastery of task. • *Sounds like* "I see that you are writing a paragraph about your favorite pastime. I really like your support sentences. One way you could improve your paragraph is to jazz up your topic sentence. Think about the example we looked at yesterday. Think about how the author in our mini-lesson started with a question as a lead."

78 THE LEARNING
COMMUNITIES
GUIDE TO
IMPROVING
READING
INSTRUCTION

HOW CAN WE ORGANIZE LITERACY INSTRUCTION THAT REFLECTS THE TEACHING-LEARNING ZONE?

Literate individuals are proficient at reading and comprehending varied texts, writing for varied purposes, and using language to communicate effectively in varied ways. Instruction that produces self-directed, literate individuals focuses on shaping student abilities in three domains of literacy: reading, writing, and language. The three-ringed model for organizing literacy instruction presented in Figure 5.6 provides a glimpse of the three domains that frame daily literacy instruction (Fountas & Pinnell, 2001; Hoyt, 2000). The model suggests possible organizational structures that teachers can use to move students from dependent learning and teacher modeling to independent learning and student application.

The reading workshop in Figure 5.7 includes shared reading, guided reading, independent reading, and literature study (Allen, 2002; Fountas & Pinnell, 2001; New Zealand Ministry of Education, 1997). *Shared reading* builds community and a love for reading when teachers read quality age-appropriate literature that appeals to all students. Shared reading nurtures student motivation to read, builds vocabulary, provides a model of fluent reading, and exposes students to information they might not read independently.

Figure 5.6   Three-Ringed Model for Organizing Literacy Instruction (Student Engagement)

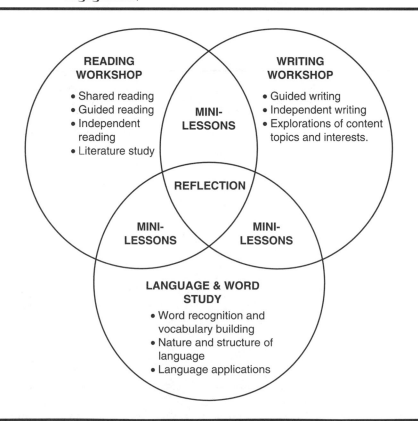

Figure 5.7   Elements of Reading Workshops

Elements	Goals	Defining Characteristics
Shared reading	<ul><li>To make age-appropriate, difficult text accessible to all readers in the classroom</li><li>To build community around reading and allow for shared discussions, investigations, and reflections</li><li>To demonstrate to students what fluent reading sounds like</li><li>To build vocabulary</li><li>To increase students' motivation to read and learn from informational text</li></ul>	<ul><li>Select brief, age-appropriate, challenging text that can be read in 10 minutes.</li><li>Use informational text for application of reading strategies to content area text.</li><li>Introduce text by discussing the title, illustrations, and author and activating prior knowledge.</li><li>Tell students the strategy that will be modeled.</li><li>Read the text aloud, modeling fluent reading.</li><li>Discuss the text after reading.</li><li>Reread text to demonstrate strategy, teach text features, and model questions good readers ask.</li><li>Encourage independent reading of text to increase comprehension, fluency, and vocabulary.</li><li>Evaluate the session by examining students' engagement and responses to the text.</li><li>Allot 20–30 minutes for shared reading session.</li></ul>
Guided reading	<ul><li>To provide as much time as possible for students to read and interact with instructional-level reading materials</li><li>To motivate and elevate the self-confidence of struggling readers</li><li>To develop independence in selecting and using appropriate reading strategies</li></ul>	<ul><li>Select text to match strengths and interests of small, homogeneous groups of students.</li><li>Plan the lesson around three phases of the reading process: before, during, and after reading.</li><li>Activate prior knowledge, talk about key vocabulary, preview text, identify a strategy to practice, and/or set purpose before reading.</li><li>Listen to students, observe reader behaviors, confirm students' problem solving, coach students in strategy use, and/or assess individual students' reading during reading.</li><li>Discuss text, invite personal responses, assess students' understanding, return to text for re-teaching, and/or extend story after reading.</li></ul>
Independent reading	<ul><li>To supplement the reading program and increase the time for reading across the school day</li><li>To increase student engagement</li></ul>	<ul><li>Conduct mini-lessons on how to select books.</li><li>Help students find materials that match interests and independent reading levels.</li><li>Organize classroom library to help students make appropriate choices.</li></ul>

(Continued)

Figure 5.7 (Continued)

Elements	Goals	Defining Characteristics
Independent reading (continued)	• Practice strategies in easy material • To promote fluency • To allow students to move at their own pace	• Support struggling readers through echo reading, choral reading, reading aloud, and so on. • Emphasize importance of rereading books and reading a range of genres. • Encourage students to write about their reading and to keep records of what they read. • Conduct conferences with individual students. • Facilitate a class meeting to share reading.
Literature study	• To accelerate the progress of struggling readers • To increase motivation to read • To teach students to think about, talk about, and write in response to high quality literature appropriate to age level • To focus on important ideas	• Provide students access to age-appropriate literature. • Model how students can lead and participate in discussions. • Monitor students' application of strategies. • Use a theme to encourage heterogeneous groups to read diverse text. • Engage groups in book talks.

Teachers differentiate reading instruction through *guided reading* using materials that are appropriate to the students' instructional levels and interests. Guided reading lessons are highly interactive, with small groups of students, so that teachers can model strategies that reflect the identified strengths and weaknesses of students. Guided reading differs from the traditional basal reading lessons because:

• Students may read different material each day, rather than all students reading the same story of the week in the grade-level basal.

• Teachers assume an active role in selecting just-right materials for homogeneous groups of students and making on-the-spot decisions about just-right instruction.

• The focus in guided reading is on acquisition and application of strategies that good readers use, rather than responding to literal questions.

• The pace for guided reading lessons is much faster than the traditional basal reading lessons.

• The role of the teacher during guided reading is that of facilitator, rather than "sage on the stage."

During *independent reading*, students are engaged in reading easy text. This allows students to read text with a high degree of accuracy and fosters fluency. Independent reading helps students develop a sense of efficacy and nurtures a desire for reading. Also, Allington documented that "differences in the volume of classroom reading were associated with elementary students' reading achievement" (Allington, 2001, p. 25). Some teachers often complain that some students do not use independent reading time appropriately or wonder if students are really reading. Accomplished teachers address this concern by reading aloud good literature and modeling enthusiasm for reading, by helping students find books that fit and match their interests, and by organizing rich classroom libraries that entice students to read. Also, they develop management and monitoring strategies for students to document what they have read and record reflections and applications of strategies. During independent reading, the teacher moves around the room, engages in conversations with individual students about what they are reading, and monitors how students are applying strategies. Another option is for the teacher to conduct a guided reading lesson with a small group while other students are reading independently.

Literature study, literature circle, and book clubs emphasize the reading of high quality literature by all students in the class, regardless of their reading ability. Teachers provide the time, materials, and structure for groups of students to think about and talk about fine literature that is age appropriate. Simulating adult book clubs, this organizational structure inspires students to read and respond critically to books that are slightly beyond their comfort level. Literature study can be theme based (e.g., stories about self, stories about families, stories about culture), concept based (e.g., change, conflict, patterns), or author based (i.e., books by the same author).

Literature study helps accelerate struggling readers' progress. Raphael (2003) describes book clubs and guided reading as the dual commitment of literacy instruction. This means that all students have access to age-appropriate literature and discussions with their peers. Student growth in reading depends on reading appropriately leveled text with teacher scaffolding. Figure 5.8 compares literature circles and guided reading.

Figure 5.8   Comparison of Literature Circles (Book Clubs) and Guided Reading

Literature Circles and Book Clubs	Guided Reading
• Use of age-appropriate text • Discussions led by students within instructional context created by the teacher • Students apply taught strategies within selected books and in discussions	• Use of instructional-level-appropriate text • Discussions led by teachers around specific skills, strategies, or words to be taught • Students learn and practice new strategies within guided reading group

82 THE LEARNING
COMMUNITIES
GUIDE TO
IMPROVING
READING
INSTRUCTION

Writer's workshop is essential to developing literacy, critical thinking, and improved reading. Yet the National Commission on Writing dubbed writing instruction as the "neglected R." Based on the 1998 National Assessment of Educational Progress (NAEP) Report, NAEP found that only one quarter of students at each grade level performed at or above the proficient level of writing (College Entrance Examination Board, 2003, p. 16). Based on this finding, NAEP recommended doubling the time students spend writing. How can this be accomplished?

Writer's workshop, which may last from thirty minutes to one hour or more, provides teachers with an instructional structure and students with varied opportunities for writing. During writer's workshop, learners are engaged in guided writing, independent writing, and inquiry writing. The focus of writer's workshop is to provide learners with opportunities to read like a writer, write like an author, and develop informational text like a researcher. Figure 5.9 provides an overview of writer's workshop (Dorn & Soffos, 2001; Fletcher & Portalupi, 1998; Fountas & Pinnell, 2001; Ray, 1999).

Exemplary literature provides the foundation for guided writing. By examining the techniques that award-winning authors use in crafting high quality literature, students can develop higher-order thinking skills, as well as apply authors' techniques to their own writing. This reading-thinking-writing connection leads to improved literacy. Ray (1999, p. 136) suggests five practices to support students' efforts:

1. Notice something about the craft of the text.

2. Talk about it and *make a theory* about why the author used that craft.

3. Give the craft a *name.*

4. Think of *other texts* that use this same craft.

5. Try to *envision* using this craft in future writing.

Young authors' writing skills can be developed through mini-lessons that focus on the craft of writing. Mini-lessons may target the whole class or small, flexible groups needing support on a particular strategy or skill. A broad range of strategies and skills, such as beginning, middle, and end or writing a strong lead, may be taught through mini-lessons that may last as few as five minutes. During mini-lessons, teachers use literature to illustrate, demonstrate, or model effective writing techniques. Students are engaged in thinking and talking about the techniques and apply those techniques to their own writing (Fletcher & Portalupi, 1998).

During *guided writing,* students also learn that quality writing involves a recursive process. This time-consuming process requires patience and includes pre-writing, drafting, revising, editing, and publishing. Teachers model, scaffold, and coach students through each of the phases.

Independent writing enables students to practice writing craft more frequently, with greater flexibility and increased fluency. Independent writing spans the curriculum as students write for a purpose in response to fiction and

⊙ **Figure 5.9** Elements of Writing Workshops

Elements	Goals	Defining Characteristics
Guided writing	• To schedule a block of time for students to work through the writing process • To provide mini-lessons of writing skills and strategies • To make students aware of the five writing stages necessary for quality writing • To provide coaching and scaffolding during the writing process • To develop writers' craft using quality literature as models for writing	• Read aloud touchstone text or quality literature to determine and apply criteria for writing. • Encourage students to read like writers. • Include mini-lessons—five to twenty minutes long, based on what students need to know to be proficient writers. • Focus on five stages: pre-writing, first draft, revision, editing, and publishing. • Find and use sources of inspiration and organize thoughts to prepare for first draft in the *pre-writing* stage. • Compose ideas on paper and focus on content, not mechanics in the *first draft* phase. • Ask students to reread, make changes, or reorganize in the *revision* stage. Writing may not need revision but may be abandoned or accepted as is. This stage is considered the most difficult stage to teach. • Proofread writing for mechanics and grammar in the *editing* stage. • Prepare writing for sharing with an audience in the *publishing* stage. • Learn about writing by studying how authors' lives impacted their writing.
Independent writing	• To provide students opportunities to write on topics of their choice • To have students explore writers' habits of mind • To allow students to explore the writing process with different genres	• Maintain on a daily basis a writer's notebook to record thoughts, responses to texts, memories, feelings, and events that might be a springboard for future writing. • Engage students in using writing to respond to literature and to aid in comprehension. • Integrate writing with all content areas whenever possible.
Inquiry writing	• To provide students the opportunity to talk, read, and write for the purpose of finding answers to questions • To engage students in learning and applying skills and tools for conducting research • To make students aware of how to gather and use varied resources • To allow students the opportunity to engage in an in-depth exploration or inquiry process	• Lead students in the process of inquiry and investigation about topics of interest. • Teach students questioning strategies as the basis for exploration and inquiry. • Provide authentic research experiences that engage students in talking, reading, and writing. • Teach students how to access varied written, oral, and technology resources. • Instruct students in using varied research tools. • Give students time to follow-through exploration over time. • Engage students in examining varied primary and secondary resources of information. • Allow students to pursue explorations during and after school hours.

expository text that is read individually or through shared reading experiences. The focus of independent writing is to enable students to develop writers' habits of mind to refine writing various genres for various purposes.

Finally, *inquiry writing* provides students with the means to record, to respond to, and to analyze investigations. Students explore problems and questions by reading, writing, and using a variety of resources. Inquiry writing provides students the opportunity to discuss, read, and write about real concepts, issues, and concerns. This type of writing takes time, requiring students to use varied resources as they apply skills and tools while investigating and writing.

Language and word study (Figure 5.10) is the third component of literacy engagement. A primary goal of word study, vocabulary building, and language structure is to spark a love of language and scaffold a bridge between vocabulary and comprehension. Language and word study should be a high priority goal to help students who lack word knowledge and word recognition strategies. When students engage in word learning, they acquire a foundation that fosters literacy development and prepares them for independent work in reading, spelling, and writing (Rice, 2003).

When students are engaged in word study, they learn specific rules, patterns, and principles of phonics and spelling that they apply in the context of their reading and writing (Fountas & Pinnell, 2001). Teachers are engaged in delivering mini-lessons, facilitating discussion about words, assessing student progress, and helping students make connections between their word choices and other words.

Vocabulary building is closely related to reading comprehension, decoding, spelling, and school achievement in general (Rice, 2003). Both vocabulary and reading comprehension are dependent on decoding, experience and world knowledge, understanding of language, and the ability to infer. Teachers engage students in reading extensively, building wall charts or word logs, and using graphic organizers to illustrate connections among words, generalizations, and patterns.

Language structure promotes oral language development and vocabulary building. Students learn how to evaluate effective use of words within the context of literature and writing. Tools may include double-entry journals, graphic organizers, semantic feature analysis, word webs, and word sorts.

WHAT SHOULD COLLABORATIVE TEAMS CONSIDER IN PLANNING EFFECTIVE INSTRUCTION?

Planning effective instruction begins with matching what the learner needs with the appropriate level of support for active engagement. Effective instruction reflects a consideration of learning experiences that target specific learning outcomes for literacy. When planning instruction, teachers can consider how to apply practices that decrease teacher-controlled instruction and increase student-scaffolded instruction by responding to eight essential questions:

Figure 5.10   Elements of Language and Word Study

Elements	Goals	Defining Characteristics
Word study	• To develop positive attitudes about words and build a strong foundation for independent use of word-recognition strategies • To build a repertoire of strategies for solving unknown words independently	• Model word-recognition strategies in the context of real reading and writing using phonemic strategies, visual strategies, meaning or morphemic strategies, linking unknown words to known words, using reference materials. • Teach word-analysis skills using word patterns, breaking words into syllables, analyzing words letter by letter. • Assess student's level of spelling to determine what the student knows and needs to know. • Analyze the form and function of words in the context of literature. • Conduct mini-lessons. • Engage students in word sorts. • Use prompts to help students figure out unknown words during reading. List some prompts on a poster.
Vocabulary building	• To provide models of quality language and literature that engage students • To connect extensive independent reading to increase vocabulary	• Provide adequate time for wide reading to support development of vocabulary. • Create wall charts to illustrate connections among words, generalizations, and patterns. • Have students keep word logs or notebooks to record new words and related rules and principles. • Implement writing workshops.
Language structure	• To promote oral language and collaboration through talking and learning together	• Evaluate effective use of words, sentences, and paragraphs in the context of literature and students' writing. • Promote student use of double-entry journals to respond to quotes or an author's use of language. • Engage small groups in creating graphic organizers and diagrams that illustrate connections among words (word webs). • Analyze semantic features.

86 THE LEARNING
COMMUNITIES
GUIDE TO
IMPROVING
READING
INSTRUCTION

1. What will students know or be able to do?

2. What comprehension strategy will I target?

3. What teaching/learning actions will take place?

4. How will students be grouped?

5. What instructional procedures will I use before reading, during reading, and after reading?

6. What will other students do if they are not working with me?

7. What evidence will indicate the progress students are making toward achieving the targeted standards, outcomes, or strategies?

8. What best practices/strategies are reflected in this lesson?

WHAT WERE THE BIG IDEAS IN THIS CHAPTER?

This chapter describes what exemplary teachers do to produce high-performing readers. Successful teachers devote adequate time for independent reading, engage students in substantive tasks, provide appropriate texts, and use modeling to demonstrate strategies good readers use. We also described brain-compatible classrooms and provided a self-assessment for creating classrooms that reflect how we learn best. The teaching-learning zone emphasizes the gradual release of responsibility and the importance of a student-scaffolded teaching style. Next, we presented a three-ring model for organizing literacy instruction and described the components of reading workshop, writing workshop, and language/word study. Finally, considerations for planning effective lessons were presented in a template that collaborative teams can use to foster student-scaffolded instruction.

CONSTRUCTIVE REFLECTION

After reading this chapter on effective teacher engagement, collaborative teams may reflect upon the key ideas and think of how to apply the concepts, practices, and strategies to instruction in their schools. Figure 5.11 presents a template that teams may use to develop, implement, analyze, and discuss lessons in a collaborative manner.

Figure 5.11   Considerations for Planning Effective Lessons

Considerations for Planning Effective Lessons
1. What will students know or be able to do?
2. What comprehension strategy will I target?
3. What teaching/learning actions will take place? ❏ Modeling ❏ Scaffolding ❏ Coaching ❏ Guided practice ❏ Independent practice
4. How will students be grouped? ❏ Whole group ❏ Cooperative groups ❏ Paired ❏ Guided reading group ❏ Literature circles or book clubs
5. What instructional procedures will I use? Before reading?   During reading?   After reading?

(Continued)

88 THE LEARNING
COMMUNITIES
GUIDE TO
IMPROVING
READING
INSTRUCTION

◉ **Figure 5.11** (Continued)

6. What will other students do if they are not working with me?

Students:

Students:

Students:

Task:

Task:

Task:

7. What evidence will indicate the progress students are making toward achieving the targeted standards, outcomes, or strategies?

8. What best practices/strategies are reflected in this lesson?

Targeting Comprehension 6

Imagine this . . .

A teacher reads aloud "Encounter" to her fourth-grade class to model how to infer and to reveal a different perspective from the traditional account presented about Columbus. "Today we continue to work on inferring as a comprehension strategy. Yesterday, we read aloud through 'Encounter' once. We noted that the author portrayed the story from the perspective of the natives and we had several questions. Today, as I re-read this book, I will pause after a couple of intriguing passages to think aloud how and what I infer. As I read, I want you to do the same." The teacher reads a short passage and pauses to think aloud. "In this passage the author says . . . and this makes me think . . . I wonder if . . .? So, I'm inferring . . ." The teacher continues to re-read the entire book, reading and pausing to think aloud. From time to time her students also discuss how and what inferences they make as the teacher reads. At the completion of the shared reading, the students select books they want to read and jot down the inferences they make on sticky notes. As the students work independently, the teacher circulates to confer with them about the inferences that they noted and coaches them when necessary.

This scenario depicts critical elements of reading instruction that results in the development of students' abilities to use comprehension strategies to make meaning of varied text. Reading is comprehending, and the dimensions of reading emphasized by the National Reading Panel (2001) were designated as crucial to reading instruction because each dimension leads to or facilitates comprehension. Phonemic awareness, phonics, fluency, vocabulary, and comprehension are inextricably linked to one another in the mission to "leave no child behind" and produce a "nation of readers" who think and read critically.

90   THE LEARNING
COMMUNITIES
GUIDE TO
IMPROVING
READING
INSTRUCTION

HOW ARE THE DIMENSIONS OF READING LINKED?

Reading experts suggest that effective instruction is systematic, explicit, and embedded within the context of authentic reading and writing (Pressley, 2002). Reading is thinking and depends on both decoding and constructing meaning. Reading is a process—it integrates higher order processes (comprehension) and lower order processes (phonemic awareness, phonics). Vocabulary and fluency aid in comprehension. A large repertoire of vocabulary facilitates readers' abilities to construct meaning from text. Moreover, when readers are able to read fluently with speed, accuracy, and expression, they can connect the ideas presented through reading more readily. This is because fluent readers do not have to concentrate on decoding the words, which frees them to focus on comprehension. Slow reading negatively impacts comprehension (Pressley, 2002).

In the primary grades, phonics is taught first, fast, and furiously using authentic reading and writing to facilitate fluency and comprehension (Adams, 1990; Juel & Minden-Cupp, 2000). Teachers do not teach phonics so that students can decode words just to get the words right—teachers teach phonics so that students can recognize words automatically in order to construct meaning (Stahl, 2001). Pressley calls phonics the way-station to comprehension and warns against the "basic skills conspiracy, where readers worry about getting the words right and the facts straight, before thinking about the 'what if's' and the 'I wonder why's'" (Pressley, 2003).

WHAT IS THE READING PROCESS AND WHAT ARE IMPLICATIONS FOR INSTRUCTION?

If reading is more than getting the words right and the facts straight, what exactly do we do when we read? You're obviously a reader or you wouldn't be reading this text. Because of your vast knowledge and experiences with teaching, you are able to make sense of what we write. But what happens when you read text that is unfamiliar and ambiguous? Read the following poem by Richard Wilbur titled *Mind* (1956). As you read, notice what you do to make meaning of the poem.

Mind in its purest play is like some bat

That beats about in caverns all alone,

Contriving by a kind of senseless wit

Not to conclude against a wall of stone.

It has no need to falter or explore;

Darkly it knows what obstacles are there,

And so may weave and flitter, dip and soar

In perfect courses through the blackest air.

And has this simile a like perfection?

The mind is like a bat. Precisely. Save

That in the very happiest intellection

A graceful error may correct the cave.

"Mind" from *Things of this World*, copyright (c) 1956 and renewed 1984 by Richard Wilbur. Reprinted by permission of Harcourt, Inc.

What is this poem about? Were you able to construct meaning? If so, what did you do to construct meaning? Did you struggle with the piece? As teachers of reading, it is important to understand the struggles of the struggling reader and the complexities of the reading process.

If you are like many adults, you may have stopped and reread the poem at certain points. Also, you may have looked for some aspect of the poem that you thought made sense to you. You probably asked questions and used the title to provide focus for your reading. You also may have connected to what you know about bats and their habitats. You possibly used these strategies and others to comprehend this poem; some of the strategies you consciously knew you were using and some you used automatically without thinking.

Good readers are active before reading, during reading, and after reading. Before reading they make predictions and overview the text. During reading, good readers revise their predictions and visualize. After reading, they summarize and evaluate the usefulness of the information in the text.

Understanding what skilled reading looks like, sounds like, and is like has implications for instruction. What are the implications? First, instruction must flow quickly from explicit modeling to independent practice. Along the way, teachers probably need to find ways to coach readers as they apply specific strategies to construct meaning in expository and fictional texts. Exemplary reading instruction also requires teachers' understanding of when and how to teach the dimensions of reading in a balanced way.

WHY SHOULD READING INSTRUCTION FOCUS ON COMPREHENSION AND VOCABULARY?

While all the dimensions of reading are important to literacy instruction, this chapter focuses on two of the dimensions where improvement is most critical—comprehension and vocabulary. Since the 1970s, research has continued to find that comprehension instruction focuses on assigning and assessing rather than explicit and active teaching of comprehension. Durkin's (1979) "mentioning study" found that teachers mentioned comprehension much more frequently than they taught it. Ongoing investigations of comprehension instruction find that although we have known for a long time what effective comprehension instruction looks like, it is not practiced in the majority of classrooms across the

United States (Pressley, 2002; Taylor & Pearson, 2002). Research also supports an emphasis on vocabulary. For one thing, children come to school with vastly different oral language and funds of word knowledge. Additionally, vocabulary knowledge is significantly related to reading comprehension, decoding, spelling, and school achievement in general (Duke, 2003; Rice, 2003).

WHAT IS THE DIFFERENCE BETWEEN SKILLS AND STRATEGIES INSTRUCTION?

Strategy is a technique that readers learn to control in order to comprehend (Duffy, 2002). Strategies instruction enables students to transfer appropriate comprehension strategies across varied texts. Let's use a tennis metaphor to differentiate between skill and strategy. A tennis player will use a number of strategies to learn how to play tennis with proficiency. Before becoming a skilled tennis player, the novice learns a number of strategies such as how to hold the racquet, hit a forehand and backhand, and serve a ball. Becoming a skilled tennis player requires years of practicing the strategies that good tennis players use, often with the help of coaches who model the strategies. Like skilled tennis players, readers learn and apply comprehension strategies in order to become skilled readers.

A pivotal difference between a strategy and a skill has to do with conscious and unconscious use (Allen, 2002). "A strategy is an intentional plan that readers use to help themselves make sense of their reading. Strategies are flexible and can be adapted to meet the demands of the reading task. Good readers use lots of strategies to help themselves make sense of text" (Tovani, 2000, p. 5). Thus, a strategy is a plan that is used consciously, and the plan is often adjusted to fit the situation (Duffy, 2003).

Conversely, a skill is something you do automatically, without thinking (Duffy, 2003). A skill is "something one obtains after the strategy has become automatic" (Allen, 2002, p. 58). Strategies instruction focuses on teaching students what the strategy is, how to use it, and when to use it in a broad array of reading contexts. Skills instruction, too frequently, relies heavily on teaching a discreet skill outside the context of literature and may not be transferable. In the past, many teachers taught comprehension through basal programs that presented a scope and sequence of skills. The teaching of skills in isolation has not helped all students apply comprehension strategies across varied texts. Figure 6.1 compares skills instruction and strategies instruction and suggests the need to move from predominant use of isolated skills instruction to predominant use of strategies instruction.

WHAT COMPREHENSION STRATEGIES DO GOOD READERS USE AND HOW CAN WE TEACH THESE STRATEGIES?

Researchers have examined what good readers do to construct meaning and have found that good readers share certain habits of mind (Blachowicz & Ogle,

◉ Figure 6.1   Comparison of Skills Instruction and Strategies Instruction

> **Moving from Isolated Skills Instruction to Strategies Instruction**

	Isolated Skills Instruction	**Strategies Instruction**
Characteristics	• Includes a scope and sequence of skills taught discretely • Focuses on knowledge of the skill • Is not embedded in authentic use • Lacks emphasis on transfer to authentic texts and contexts	• Spirals across grades and different texts • Focuses on application and use of the strategy • Emphasizes how-to knowledge • Transfers to authentic texts and contexts
Procedures for teaching and assessing	• Uses worksheets and workbooks • Gives a definition or example of the skill • Provides directions that students follow with little or no modeling • Assesses students using multiple choice and/or short answer tests	• Uses varied genres of expository and fictional literature • Embeds authentic reading and writing across the curriculum • Describes explicitly what the strategy is, how to use it, and when to use it • Moves on a teaching-learning continuum from modeling to independent practice • Emphasizes modeling in read alouds, think alouds, guided practice, reflection, and independent application • Assesses student application through observation of oral and written responses to text
Example	• Teachers give students a worksheet and ask them to sequence sentence strips that describe the order of events in a story	• Teacher reads aloud a picture book and models how to use questions to understand text by thinking aloud

2001; Pressley, 1999, 2002). Before reading, good readers identify a specific purpose for reading, peruse the text, and anticipate what the text might be about by using prior knowledge. During reading, good readers relate their prior predictions to what the text says and read the text from front to back, sometimes reading ahead or looking back for clarification. Proficient readers may also slow down during their reading when the text is difficult or when the passage pertains to their reading goals. They continue to predict and question the author during reading. After reading, good readers reflect on ideas in the text relative to their prior knowledge, summarize the ideas, and evaluate the usefulness of the information.

In general, good readers share the ability to flexibly use specific comprehension strategies. The goal of comprehension instruction is to help students become self-regulated and independent readers. The good news is that students' meaning making can be improved by teaching the following evidence-based comprehension strategies (Harvey & Goudvis, 2000; Keene & Zimmerman, 1997; Pearson, Roehler, Dolle, & Duffy, 1992):

- Using schema to make connections between what they know or have experienced and new information presented in text

- Asking questions of themselves, the authors they encounter, and the texts they read

- Making inferences during and after reading

- Distinguishing importance in text and identifying themes

- Monitoring or clarifying understanding of text

- Visualizing and creating images to facilitate understanding

- Synthesizing or summarizing information

"Teaching students to articulate comprehension strategies is essential in reading programs based on best practices" (Pressley, 1999, p. 92), and effective strategies instruction involves specific instructional practices and procedures. Pressley (2002) recommended that teachers devote a great deal of time teaching each strategy one at a time, using a wide variety of high-quality fiction and nonfiction. Learning how to apply strategies takes time; thus strategies instruction is ongoing and spans a lifetime of learning. Good teachers of comprehension strategies are users of comprehension strategies and make their use of strategies evident to their students.

What does effective strategies instruction look like? It reflects a set of teacher actions that focus on explaining what the strategy consists of, why the strategy is important, when the strategy should be used, and how to apply the strategy. Researchers generally agree that strategies instruction is most effective when taught explicitly and directly using the following procedure (Beers, 2003; Duffy, 2002; Harvey & Goudvis, 2000; Palinscar & Brown, 1984; Paris, Lipson, & Wixon, 1983; Pressley, 1999):

- Begin with identifying the strategy necessary to comprehend a particular text that you select.

- Explain to the students what strategy you will model while reading, why the strategy is important or why good readers use the strategy, and when to use the strategy in actual reading.

- Read the text, pausing to think aloud and model how to perform the strategy.

- Engage students in whole group, small group, and paired discussions about strategy use.

- Provide students with multiple real-reading opportunities and materials to practice the strategy.

- Observe students' attempts and scaffold use as needed.

- Assess both students' strategy use and comprehension of content.

- Give students opportunities to use strategy independently in authentic reading experiences.

Mini-lessons provide the foundation for strategies instruction. These instructional powerhouses last from five to fifteen minutes during which teachers model strategy use. Although short in duration, mini-lessons are packed with explicit and timely responses to specific student needs. Figure 6.2 provides a sample mini-lesson on schema to make connections.

Essential elements of each comprehension strategy are presented in light of what teachers can do to support comprehension of text. Keep in mind that in order to help struggling readers become independent, proficient readers, "we need to differentiate between *instruction* and *instructions*" (Beers, 2003, p. 47). In other words, struggling readers need ongoing, concrete instruction that demonstrates how to apply each strategy. This instruction goes beyond reading the instructions or directions found on most worksheets.

Using Schema to Make Connections

Good readers use schema to relate to unfamiliar text. Schema are the sum total of background knowledge, previous experiences, emotions, and understandings brought to any learning situation. Schema impact what we learn (Harvey & Goudvis, 2000). Three forms of schema, or ways of accessing prior knowledge and experiences, aid in constructing meaning: (1) text-to-self, (2) text-to-text, and (3) text-to-world. *Text-to-self connections* occur when readers make connections between the text and their own experiences and memories (Keene & Zimmerman, 1997; Harvey & Goudvis, 2000; Tovani, 2000). *Text-to-text connections* occur when the reader compares two or more texts. The reader may compare the plot, content, structure, or style of different texts. *Text-to-world connections* happen when the reader considers facts or other information about the world to information in the text. Readers also may use schema involving what they know about particular authors to understand a text.

96 THE LEARNING
COMMUNITIES
GUIDE TO
IMPROVING
READING
INSTRUCTION

Modeling how to use schema emphasizes two key processes: (1) how readers use their own knowledge or experience to understand text and (2) how a reader's schema are changed by what was read (Keene & Zimmerman, 1997). To illustrate this process, we include a think aloud for *Mind*, presented earlier in this chapter.

"Mind in its purest play is like some bat/that beats about in caverns all alone,/contriving by a kind of senseless wit/not to conclude against a wall of stone." *"I know bats live in caverns so I guess the poem is comparing the brain with bats. I remember the saying 'blind as a bat' and know that bats use their senses to avoid flying into things."*

"It has no need to falter or explore;/darkly it knows what obstacles are there,/and so may weave and flitter, dip and soar/in perfect courses through the blackest air." *"I'm not quite sure if this means the mind is wandering like daydreaming or skipping from one topic to another! I think the author believes the mind is like a bat because the mind knows it has limitations or boundaries like a cave."*

"And has this simile a like perfection?/The mind is like a bat. Precisely. Save/that in the very happiest intellection/a graceful error may correct the cave." *"Well, the author repeats that the mind is like a bat, 'save'—that means except—in the best and brightest thinking a mistake could change the mind's boundaries. So, maybe I was wrong; perhaps the author is saying that the mind does not have limitations like a bat's cave."*

In addition to think alouds, graphic organizers can serve as scaffolds for teaching and learning strategies. Using a graphic organizer such as the schema chart, students can learn to make connections to text evident as illustrated in the mini-lesson in Figure 6.2.

Asking Questions of Themselves, the Authors They Encounter, and the Texts They Read

Good readers ask questions to help them focus and make meaning of a text. Effective readers ask varied questions, depending on the information needed for comprehension. They generally ask four types of questions: (1) to clarify meaning; (2) to predict about text; (3) to interact with the author's style, content, or format; and (4) to find a specific answer in text. In particular, teachers must model and emphasize the role of asking questions during reading. Teachers also should encourage students to use higher-level thinking questions and can do so by helping them to ask "fat" and "skinny" questions (Fogarty, 2001, p. 91). Skinny questions are those that have only one possible answer, and fat questions are those that allow for many diverse responses. Teachers also can post question charts, like the one in Figure 6.3 that students can refer to when applying the questioning strategy during reading (Allington, 2001; Beers, 2003).

Making Inferences During and After Reading

An inference is "the ability to connect what is in the text with what is in the mind to create an educated guess" (Beers, 2003, p. 62). Inferencing is reading between the lines or is the "bedrock of comprehension, not only in

◉ Figure 6.2   Sample Mini-Lesson on Using Schema to Make Connections

Purpose: Modeling how to use schema to make connections and make meaning of text

Text/resource: *Grass* by Carl Sandburg

Pile the bodies high at Austerlitz and Waterloo
Shovel them under and let me work-
I am the grass; I cover all.

And pile them high at Gettysburg.
And pile them high at Ypres and Verdun.
Shovel them under and let me work.

Two years, ten years and the
Passengers ask the conductor:
What place is this?
Where are we now?
I am the grass.
Let me work.

What the teacher will do:

- Read once through the poem *Grass* to familiarize students with the text and for enjoyment.
- Prepare students for the second reading of the poem by explaining that you will demonstrate what good readers do by thinking aloud. Tell them you will use your schema to make three types of connections: text-to-self, text-to-text, and text-to-world. This strategy helps readers make meaning with all text. Describe the three types of connections and tell students that as you read and think aloud, you want them to listen to the types of connections you make.
- Present the graphic organizer for noting schema and explain how to use the chart.

Text-to-Self
Text-to-Text
Text-to-World

- Read through the poem a stanza at a time and think aloud how you make text-to-self, text-to-text, and text-to-world connections to comprehend the poem's meaning. As you do this, write the connections in the appropriate places on the chart.
- The following chart reveals how schema could be modeled as an aid for comprehending the first stanza of the text. Words in italics indicate the portion of the poem used. Deconstruct the first stanza.

Text-to-Self
Text-to-Text
Text-to-World

Shovel them under and let me work-I am the grass; I cover all.

"I once watched some men prepare a layer of sod. It was amazing how they could lift the sod and you could see all these little bugs and worms underneath. I can see how grass can cover up so much. Is the grass used to cover up the bodies?"

Pile the bodies high at Austerlitz and Waterloo

"I remember that in the book *The Secret Lives of Bees*, when May was upset she would pile up rocks. Is this how the bodies were piled? If so, this seems horrible."

Pile the bodies high at Austerlitz and Waterloo

"This reminds me that recently in Iraq they found mass graves of people who had been killed. I wonder how many people were killed at Austerlitz and Waterloo."

What the students will do:

- Listen to teacher read aloud and think aloud the poem.
- Observe how the teacher uses the schema chart.
- Discuss how connections and schema aided comprehension.
- Use the schema or making connections chart with a book of their choice.
- Discuss the connections with the teacher and other students.

98 THE LEARNING
COMMUNITIES
GUIDE TO
IMPROVING
READING
INSTRUCTION

Figure 6.3   Question Stems and Purpose

Question Stem	Purpose
• Why . . . ? • Who is . . . ? • What does this section (fill in detail) mean? • I don't get this part here . . . • What's this part about?	Clarify meaning
• What would happen if . . . ? • Do you think that . . . ? • How is this (fill in detail) like this (fill in detail)?	Predict about text
• Why did the author begin by . . . ? • What is the author's saying? • How can I use the author's illustration?	To interact with the author's style, content, or format
• What does this (person, place, thing) look like? • What does this text teach me about (fill in theme) . . . ? • What has happened so far?	Find a specific answer in text

reading . . . inferring is about reading faces, reading body language, reading expressions, and reading tone, as well as reading text" (Harvey & Goudvis, 2000, p. 105). We infer when we use prior knowledge and information in the text to (1) draw conclusions, (2) make predictions, (3) form ongoing interpretations, (4) combine background knowledge and explicitly stated information from text to answer questions, and (5) make critical judgments (Keene & Zimmerman, 1997). Proficient readers use a variety of inferences to understand text. Teachers can model and scaffold the use of varied inferences (Beers, 2003). Figure 6.4 summarizes the types of inferences and comments teachers can make. Post inference types on chart paper and refer to them daily while reading aloud short passages or poems. The left column presents nine types of inferences that good readers make. The right column provides sample comments and questions teachers can use to encourage students to infer.

Another strategy for teaching inferencing incorporates syntax and inferring. The teacher performs *syntax surgery* using a passage on the overhead (Beers, 2003). During the syntax surgery mini-lesson, the teacher models how to infer by thinking aloud and using visual cues to show relationships between words or phrases and inferences. For syntax surgery, teachers:

- Copy a section or paragraph from a textbook, trade book, poem, or article onto a transparency.

- Think aloud as you read the section.

Figure 6.4 Types of Inferences and Comments That Teachers Can Make

Type of Inference	Comments Teachers Can Make
Relate the text to their prior knowledge and experiences.	What would you do?
Recognize the antecedents for pronouns.	Look for pronouns and figure out what to connect them to.
Figure out the meaning of unknown words from context clues.	Look for words you don't know and see if any of the other words in the sentence or surrounding sentences can give you an idea of what those unknown words mean.
Understand the tone of characters' words.	Look at how the character said . . . How would you have interpreted what that character said if he had said . . . ?
Identify characters' beliefs, personalities, and motivations.	After you read this section, think about why the character acted this way.
Understand characters' relationships to one another.	Think about how (character's name) will react when he finds out what (another character's name) did.
Provide details about the setting.	What details can you add to this setting?
Provide explanations or details regarding events or ideas presented in the text.	What is a possible explanation for this event (idea, detail)?
Recognize author's biases and view of the world.	What do you think is the author's underlying motivation or beliefs?

SOURCE: Beers (2003)

- Connect the words that are related using circles, lines, colors, or arrows.

- Show how pronouns, nouns, and signal words (i.e., sequence words, words that compare and contrast) help construct meaning.

Distinguishing Importance in Text and Identifying Themes

Good readers make decisions about what is important in text. This strategy is most often associated with informational text; however, good readers also use this strategy when identifying underlying themes in fiction. A theme is "the idea that holds the story together, such as a comment about either society, human nature, or the human condition" (Williams, 2002, p. 128).

In identifying what is most important, readers use a two-step process (Duffy, 2003). First, readers actively question the author, looking for clues about what is important. Second, readers think about how the clues go together to determine the most important idea.

100 THE LEARNING
COMMUNITIES
GUIDE TO
IMPROVING
READING
INSTRUCTION

Within this two-step process, readers use three levels of cues from text: word level, sentence level, and text level (Keene & Zimmerman, 1997). At the *word level*, readers identify words that connect ideas such as *and, but, for, nor,* and *yet*. Readers also note words that seem to highlight the overall meaning of the text. At the *sentence level*, readers look for key sentences that emphasize critical ideas and often begin or end the passage in nonfiction. At the *text level*, readers constantly revise their opinions about what is most important, not coming to conclusions until they complete reading and reflecting upon the text. At each of the levels, decisions about what is most important are impacted by the reader's

- Purpose

- Prior knowledge about text content

- Beliefs, opinions, and experiences

- Knowledge of and experience with text features

- Concepts that another reader mentions prior to, during, or after reading (Keene & Zimmerman, 1997).

Teachers can help students learn this strategy in several ways. First, teachers can model and think aloud what is most important using short passages and identifying key words and sentences that provide clues. Teachers can show students how to use highlighters or sticky notes for identifying key ideas. Since expository text has particular features that help or hinder the process of identifying the most important ideas, teachers must demonstrate how to overview a text noting features such as titles, text organizers, subheadings, fonts, graphics, tables, and illustrations (Harvey & Goudvis, 2000).

Visualizing and Creating
Images to Facilitate Understanding

We've heard the adage "a picture is worth a thousand words" and we have experienced the benefits of visuals a number of times in our lifetimes. For example, when we have to hook up that three-in-one copier, fax, and printer and we are technology challenged, we really appreciate that picture or diagram provided in the instructions. Visualization is the movie of the mind that propels Olympic competitors toward the gold and is a comprehension strategy that helps readers. "An image, like a paint stroke, means little alone but becomes a memory associated with a text in the mind of a reader" (Keene & Zimmerman, 1997, p. 126). When proficient readers read, they form mental pictures of what is being read that help them construct meaning. As students visualize, they

- Recall a sequence of information

- Become immersed in the rich details of the text, which enables them to recall these details more easily

- Engage all the senses and emotions to activate prior knowledge

- Use images to draw conclusions

- Adjust their images as they read to summarize what is read

- Imagine application possibilities

- Realize joy from reading (Keene & Zimmerman, 1997; Harvey & Goudvis, 2000; Robb, 2003)

Effective visualization instruction includes teacher modeling of the strategy using real text and student practice with creating mental pictures while reading. Practice should integrate the use with both expository text and fiction. For example, when students read a text about the life cycle of a butterfly, ask them to stop and mentally illustrate what they read.

Another effective learning experience is "sketch to stretch" (Beers, 2003, pp. 172–173). Students work by themselves or with a partner to create representative sketches of text interpretations. On the back of their sketches, students write an explanation. Next, students share their sketches with small groups that respond to the sketches before hearing the students' explanations.

Synthesizing or Summarizing Information

A true synthesis is an "Aha!" or "light bulb occurrence" that is constructed over time (Harvey & Goudvis, 2000). Synthesis is thinking in progress and is considered the most difficult strategy to learn because it is a combination of all the other comprehension strategies. Proficient readers synthesize during reading and after reading. During reading, readers synthesize when they

- Monitor overall meaning, concepts, and themes

- Interact personally with text through interactive questioning

- Use knowledge of patterns and styles in expository and fictional text

- Paraphrase and summarize what they have read

- Pay attention to story elements such as setting, theme, and characters to make decisions about overall meaning

- Revise previous decisions as they encounter new information (Harvey & Goudvis, 2000; Keene & Zimmerman, 1997)

After reading, readers synthesize as they

- Retell the relevant ideas and themes succinctly

- Share, recommend, and critically review books (Keene & Zimmerman, 1997)

Teachers can assist students with synthesizing in a variety of ways. A basic framework for retelling that students can use to synthesize involves three considerations: (1) What is important about what I read? (2) How can I tell what is important in a way that makes sense? (3) Did I tell too much or too little? After reading a story, teachers can demonstrate how to use these questions to summarize information in the story. This process is brief, but occasionally the teacher might consider recording her synthesized ideas on chart paper or sticky notes (Harvey & Goudvis, 2000). Figure 6.5 provides a mini-lesson on summarizing information.

Monitoring or Clarifying Understanding of Text

Proficient readers use a variety of fix up strategies when they do not understand a text. Think about it. You are reading a newspaper article on a Saturday morning when all of a sudden you realize you do not know what you have read. You don't have a clue what you have read because you have "spaced out" while reading. Students need to understand that all readers do this from time to time and what they can do about it. Teachers can help students by providing explicit instruction that encourages them to (1) be conscious of what they are thinking when they read, (2) recognize confusion and obstacles that get in the way of understanding, and (3) fix meaning when it eludes them (Harvey & Goudvis, 2000; Tovani, 2000).

To fix comprehension, good readers are cognizant of which strategies to activate and know how to automatically apply those strategies. To promote student use of fix up strategies, teachers can create a poster or bookmarks that list the possibilities. The list can encourage students to

- Write down or talk about their thinking

- Observe when focus is lost

- Stop and think about what was already read

- Reread

- Retell

- Read ahead

- Identify what is confusing about the text

- Ask questions and try to find the answers

- Use table of contents, indexes, subheadings, bold or italicized words, pictures, graphs, and illustrations

- Make a prediction about the text

- Visualize what was read

- Make connections to self, text, and world

- Match the difficulty with the strategy that will best solve it

- Change reading rate—slow down or speed up (Harvey & Goudvis, 2000; Tovani, 2000)

Figure 6.5 Mini-Lesson on Synthesizing or Summarizing

Purpose: Modeling how to summarize to make meaning of text

Harriet Tubman

Born a slave around 1820,
Harriet Tubman didn't go to school,
Worked in the fields
And was almost killed.

She escaped from slavery
On the Underground Railroad,
Became a conductor known as "Moses"
And braved slave hunters and perilous trips to the South.

Following the North Star by night
She led 300 slaves North to freedom claiming,
"I never ran my train off the track,
and I never lost a passenger."

What the teacher will do:

- Read once through the poem *Harriet Tubman* to familiarize students with the text and for enjoyment.
- Prepare students for the second reading of the poem by explaining that you will demonstrate how good readers summarize.
- Present the framework *Somebody Wanted But So* (Beers, 2003) and explain how the framework can help them to write a sentence that summarizes the poem. This framework can be used with fiction. Explain the following steps for using this strategy: (1) Identify which *somebody* or main character, (2) identify what somebody *wanted*, (3) *but* represents what problem occurred, and (4) *so* represents what happened finally.
- Tell students that when they are using this organizer with long pieces of text, they need to break the text into chunks and use connecting words such as *and, but, later, and then.*
- This graphic organizer helps students with point of view when they write statements about multiple somebodies or characters.

Somebody	Wanted	But	So

- Read through the poem and think aloud how to use the graphic organizer to summarize. As you do this, write the phrases on the graphic organizer.
- The following chart reveals a possible summary statement for the poem.

Somebody	Wanted	But	So
Harriet Tubman	*Wanted* to free her people	*But* the Civil War made it dangerous	*So* she organized the Underground Railroad and never lost a passenger.

(Continued)

104 THE LEARNING
COMMUNITIES
GUIDE TO
IMPROVING
READING
INSTRUCTION

◉ **Figure 6.5** (Continued)

What the students will do:

- Listen to the teacher read aloud the poem and model how to summarize.
- Observe how the teacher uses the *Somebody Wanted But So* framework.
- Create summaries by using the *Somebody Wanted But So* framework with books of their choice.
- Share the summaries with the teacher and other students.

To summarize, "comprehension is both a product and a process, something that requires purposeful, strategic effort on the reader's part" (Beers, 2003, p. 45). Therefore, effective comprehension instruction

- Takes place over time and is an evolving process

- Balances comprehension with decoding, word recognition, vocabulary building, fluency, and response to literature

- Is embedded in rich, varied literature

- Emphasizes the development of thinking skills necessary for comprehension

- Provides students with ample opportunities for reading, writing, and talking about text

- Fosters the development of self-regulated and independent readers

- Emphasizes explicit teaching or modeling of comprehension strategies

The next section focuses on vocabulary building, a partner to comprehension. This section presents nine intervention tools and describes the teacher's role in vocabulary development.

HOW CAN WE TEACH VOCABULARY TO IMPROVE COMPREHENSION?

"Word knowledge is one of the most powerful predictors of reading comprehension" (Rasinski et al., 2000, p. 1). Vocabulary plays a critical part in comprehension, as readers cannot comprehend what they read unless they know what most of the words mean. However, direct instruction in word meanings will not significantly reduce the gap between students with poor and rich vocabularies (Baker, Simmons, & Kameenui, 1995). Students who struggle to read, "with poor vocabularies, including diverse learners, need strong and systematic educational support to become successful independent word learners" (p. 7). Research confirms the ineffectiveness of traditional approaches to vocabulary instruction such as finding and writing definitions or drill-and-practice that involves multiple repetitions of words and their definitions (Stahl & Fairbanks, 1986).

Teachers need to be selective in the vocabulary they directly teach because students learn most of the words they know indirectly, and texts that students read have too many unfamiliar words for direct instruction. What should teachers consider in planning vocabulary instruction in light of the diverse needs of students?

We know students learn vocabulary in different ways: through incidental word learning, teacher-supported word learning, intentional word learning, and application of word learning activities. *Incidental word learning* has to do with how we naturally or indirectly learn words in the context of everyday living (Rice, 2003). In fact, children learn about 3,000 words a year, but only about 300 from organized instruction (Beck & McKeown, 1999). Teachers can support incidental word learning by encouraging independent reading, supporting opportunities for abundant talk in the classroom, reading passages or books aloud to students, engaging students in book discussions, playing word games, and using think alouds to demonstrate how to use context clues (Allen, 2002; Rice, 2003). The most important thing teachers can do to promote vocabulary growth is to increase students' volume of reading (Nagy, 1988).

Several factors may affect incidental word learning, and "inconsiderate text" is a factor that presents obstacles for struggling readers. Struggling students need more support to comprehend inconsiderate texts. Inconsiderate texts are those that have

- Excessive numbers or types of new words

- Unclear referents

- Irrelevant information

- Challenging vocabulary undefined in context

- Dense information

- Poor organization of ideas

- Overestimated prior knowledge expectations (Moje, 2003)

Teacher-supported word learning occurs during instruction (Rice, 2003). For example, the class might talk about words during a read aloud or shared reading, or may engage in analogy instruction. Another teacher-supported word learning component is the exploration of words. During word exploration, students focus on how words work, what they mean, and how they are used (Rasinski et al., 2000). By exploring words, students develop a greater appreciation of words and consider how to use words when reading, writing, and speaking.

Intentional word learning occurs as students study words in texts or learn content-area terms (Rice, 2003). This reading-embedded way of learning words crosses subject areas as students learn vocabulary related to informational text they read.

Finally, students apply word-learning strategies naturally as they read (Rice, 2003). Repeated application of specific word-learning strategies during independent reading develops students' confidence in using a broad range of words fluently and flexibly.

In summary, vocabulary instruction should decrease the practice of looking up definitions, asking students to write sentences for words they do not know, or relying on context for comprehension (Allen, 2003). Instead, teachers should increase the time for reading; create language-rich environments for reading, writing, and talking; and vary the level of direct instruction for diverse learners. The next section describes ten simple, research-based intervention tools that teachers can examine to provide teacher-supported and intentional word learning opportunities across classes. These strategies can serve as alternatives to vocabulary worksheets and definition writing and can provide a scaffold for teaching and learning vocabulary in more engaging ways.

Intervention Tool #1: Technical Terms and Vocabulary Cards (Moje, 2003)

The purpose of technical vocabulary cards is to support comprehension of technical concepts in expository text. Directions for students include:

- Using 5 × 7 cards, write a word on one side and draw lines on the other side to create four quadrants. Label the quadrants (1) what it is, (2) what it is not, (3) example, and (4) reader/dictionary definition.

What it is . . .	What it is not . . .
Example . . .	Reader/dictionary definition . . .

- Start with the dictionary and write a definition of the word in your own words.

- Describe what it is in the next quadrant by writing characteristics of the word and then write what it is not.

- List examples of the concept or word in the last quadrant.

- Maintain a "living" vocabulary collection by punching a hole in the corner of the cards and filing the cards on a metal ring.

Intervention Tool #2: Found Poems (Worthy et al., 2001)

The purpose of found poems is to help students appreciate beautiful language and powerful words. Students find strong words in a passage and use those words to create a poem. Directions for students include:

- Select one or two paragraphs from a story or trade book that describes a character or setting.

- Look for strong verbs and nouns and circle the strongest words; cross out unnecessary or repetitive words.

- Keep the words in the author's order and write a poem using the strongest words. Think about the meaning of the poem and consider where to make line breaks and which words can be emphasized through repetition.

- Edit and check the poem for verb tense and meaning. Title the poem.

- Write the final draft and cite the original source (author, title, publication information, page numbers).

Intervention Tool #3: Anticipating Words (Allen, 2002)

Anticipating words gives students a strategy for activating background knowledge prior to reading, helps students make connections among words, and reinforces reading for a purpose or strategic reading. Directions for students include:

- Identify words in expository text that may represent barriers to students' comprehension and write the beginning letter of these words in a list.

- Give students the title of the text or an illustration and the list of the beginning letters of selected words. Tell students that the letters represent words that are important to understanding the text and are clues for predicting words they will find in the article.

- In small groups, students brainstorm words they predict they will see in the poem and record their words in journals, on individual 3 × 5 cards for each letter, or on charts.

- Students share their words before reading the text, return to their lists after reading the text to compare their words with words they encountered in the text, and then discuss words from their lists that could be substituted in the text.

Intervention Tool #4: Word Sorts (Fountas & Pinnell, 2001)

Word sorting enables students to form hypotheses and generalizations about the properties of words and link new words to words they know and can spell. Students analyze features of words and sort them into either open or closed categories. Directions for students include:

- Identify words that fit the feature that you want to emphasize and write the words on cards.

- Students work with partners to review word cards and look for words that have like or shared features, identify these features, and sort words into categories (open category sort). One student can sort the words and the other student can guess the category.

- Words can be sorted by spelling, sound, or meaning.

- For closed sorts, the teacher assigns the categories and gives students key words to head each category. Students sort the other words under the key word columns.

- Students discuss the final sorting of words and check their work.

- Variations on word sorting can include multiple sorts of the same words with different categories, speed sorts to build processing skills, and written sorts where students write words in columns

Intervention Tool #5: Vocabulary Sort and Story Prediction (Robb, 2003)

This strategy activates and enlarges prior knowledge of vocabulary words before reading a selection and sets a purpose for reading. Directions include:

- Before a shared reading, give students the title of a text and a list of 12–17 words and phrases from the text. Ask students (in small groups) to think about what the story or poem could be about.

- Students sort the words according to which labels they think the words fit most appropriately: characters, problem, or outcome. A word may be used only once.

- Then students use the words to write a "gist" statement that depicts a possible scenario or gist of the story. Students share their predictions before reading the text.

- Last, students read the text to test their predictions and then discuss the gist of the story and their predictions.

Intervention Tool #6: Semantic Feature Analysis (Johnson & Pearson, 1984)

This strategy helps students comprehend word meanings and concepts by comparing the word's features to those of other words with similar or opposite meanings. Directions include:

- Select a general category of study such as sports or animals. Create a matrix for key vocabulary terms or concepts to be written vertically down the left margin of the matrix. Features of the key words will be written horizontally across the top column of the matrix.

- List several words that fit the category in the first column and elicit other words from students.

- List features that the words might share across the top of the matrix and invite students to add to this list.

- Students mark a plus sign (+) or a minus sign (–) to indicate whether or not the words listed down the left column share the same feature. Students mark a question mark if they don't know if a word has a feature or not. See sample below.

Intervention Tool #6: Sample Semantic Feature Analysis

- Students explain the reasoning of their marks to other students.

Animal	Herbivore?	Carnivore?	Omnivore?
Shark	–	+	–
Eagle	–	+	–
Rabbit	+	–	–
Giraffe	+	–	–
Bear	–	–	+
Cow	+	–	–
Baboon	–	–	+
Hyena	–	+	–
Catfish	–	–	+
Squirrel	+	–	–

Intervention Tool #7: Analogy Instruction (HuffBenkoski & Greenwood, 1995)

Analogy instruction builds vocabulary, comprehension, and conceptual relationships across the curriculum. Class discussions provide the foundation for analogy development. When students discuss their reasons for word selection in completing analogies, they increase their vocabulary. These discussions help students see nuances of meaning. Directions include:

- The teacher draws two objects on a board (e.g., a hat and a coat) and asks how the two objects are the same (they both keep parts of the body warm).

- The teacher asks relational questions about the objects. (On what part of the body do you wear a hat? On what part of the body do you wear a coat?)

- The teacher writes an analogous statement (a hat is to the head as a coat is to the body) and tells the students that this statement is an analogy.

- This process is repeated as the teacher models and thinks aloud analogies.

- At times, the order of the pairs is reversed to teach the role that sequence plays in making analogies.

- The teacher provides students with four words and asks students to determine which one does not belong. The list of words includes some vocabulary words that have been introduced previously.

- A discussion follows during which students provide divergent reasons for why certain words do not belong.

- Students are given three word groups and are asked to provide their own word that would belong to each group.

- The thinking processes for word selection are discussed so that students begin to see that there are many correct answers but that some answers may be more precise than others. For example, students may be given the words *bathing suit, shorts,* and *sandals.* They might add the word *sweater* to the list, thinking that the grouping has to do with clothing. While sweater might not be an incorrect word, discussion would lead students to find that *tank top* might be a better word because it is part of summer clothing.

- Students state the relationship between two words by creating stem or bridge sentences (e.g., igloo and ice). The two words are used to produce a sentence that states the relationship between the two words, keeping them in order (e.g., an igloo is made of ice).

- Students provide words for three-part analogies, such as "eye is to seeing as ear is to_____" or "feather is to bird as _____is to fish."

- Students play a game by creating three-part analogies in cooperative groups and having other students determine words to insert.

- Students create analogies independently.

Intervention Tool #8: Word Storm (Kemp, 1994)

Word storms allow students to contrast the use of vocabulary words in relationship to their thoughts about the usefulness of word application. A word storm helps build a community of learners and is highly interactive. This tool may be used as a pre-teaching learning experience to familiarize students with informational text vocabulary. Directions:

- Students work in pairs or small groups.

- Words are divided among the groups so that no more than two groups have the same word. Duplication of words enables students to distinguish varied uses of words.

- Groups use a word storm sheet, and their task is to respond to each prompt, in any order.

- For example, in response to the prompt "What are some different forms of the word?" students may respond with different parts of speech, synonyms, or tense variations.

- Students may experience difficulty in responding to some prompts for some of the words. This helps students understand that words possess different qualities and are inconsistent in usage.

- Groups work together on one day and report their responses to the class on successive days.

Word Storm Sheet

To understand a word, it is sometimes better to know more than just the dictionary definition. A word map lets you write down different types of information to help you understand what a word means and the many ways in which the word can be used.

What is the word?

Write the sentence from the text in which the word is used.

What are some different forms of the word?

Name three people who would be most likely to use the word besides teachers.

What are some other ways of saying the same thing?

Make up a sentence using this word. Let your sentence tell what the word means.

- Groups may use dictionaries, glossaries, thesauruses, or their own knowledge for the word information search.

- Some categories are ambiguous, allowing students to respond in various ways.

Intervention Tool #9: Vocabulary Web Model

Vocabulary webs enable students to attain an in-depth understanding of interesting words. Webs also allow students to process challenging and interesting words. Directions:

- Teacher completes a vocabulary web with the whole class.

- Students work in groups to use the vocabulary web with other words found in text selections.

- Students may extend the web by adding extensions to the main circles.

- Once familiar with the vocabulary web, students can use a streamlined version when encountering new words.

SOURCE: Center for Gifted Education (1999)

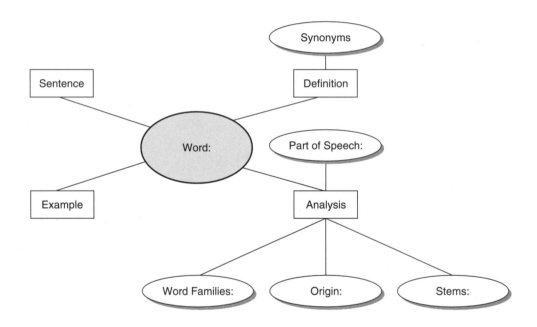

There are numerous ways that teachers can build students' word knowledge and vocabulary, but the best way is "through plenty of authentic contextual reading" (Rasinski et al., 2000, p. 1). This is because students' sight word vocabulary is increased by frequent and repeated encounters with words. Also, students come across a variety of new words as they read, and by reading these words in literature they learn new words and concepts. While word learning by reading is desirable, teachers should consider that some students may have difficulty learning words from reading, especially if they have limited metacognitive abilities, motivation, reasoning abilities (especially inferencing), awareness of sentence/text structure, and domain knowledge (Rice, 2003). Figure 6.6 summarizes considerations for planning effective vocabulary instruction.

◎ Figure 6.6   The Big Ideas of Effective Vocabulary Instruction

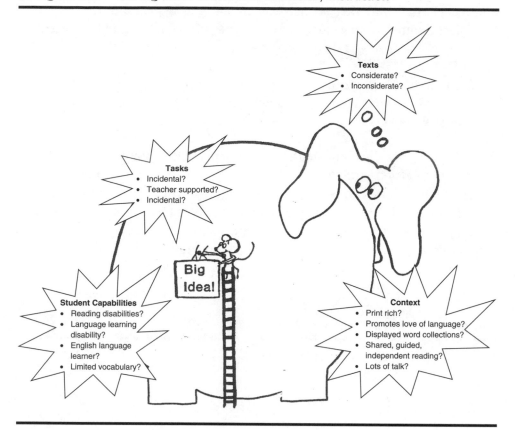

WHAT WERE THE BIG IDEAS IN THIS CHAPTER?

Chapter 6 presented research-based strategies for teaching comprehension and vocabulary. We began with a description of the reading process and we described the difference between skills instruction and strategies instruction. Seven research-based comprehension strategies were explained: (1) using schema to make connections, (2) asking questions, (3) making inferences, (4) distinguishing importance in text and identifying themes, (5) monitoring or clarifying understanding, (6) visualizing and creating images, and (7) synthesizing or summarizing information. Also, two mini-lessons for comprehension were included. Finally, we linked vocabulary to comprehension and provided nine intervention tools for building vocabulary. Collaborative teams can support growth in practice by carefully comparing current instruction to the research-based practices described in this chapter.

CONSTRUCTIVE REFLECTIONS

1. As a team, use the prompts below to select three passages from this chapter. Discuss your responses with your instructional team.

Review the chapter and select a passage in this chapter that *squares* off with your beliefs and share this passage with a colleague, explaining why.

Select another passage in this chapter that is *circling* around in your mind. Share your response and the underlying reasons you selected the passage that you did.

Select a third passage in this chapter that you think makes the most important *point*. Share your response and why you think this is the most important point of the chapter.

2. Teams may use the template in Figure 6.7 to create a mini-lesson for one of the comprehension strategies. Team members independently implement the lesson and collect student work samples to share during a follow-up discussion with the team. During the discussion, team members talk about what went well with the lesson, what they would do differently the next time, and how students responded to the lesson. Teachers may also keep a reflective journal of comprehension lessons.

Figure 6.7   Mini-Lesson Template

Strategy:
Purpose:
Text/resource(s):
What the teacher will do: • • •
What the students will do: • • •

Creating Professional Learning Communities for Literacy

7

Imagine this . . .

Once upon a time there was a school that had four principals in five years. Student achievement was very poor, staff morale was abysmal, and parents were passive. Closed classroom doors hid bored students who labored over an endless sea of worksheets and teachers who struggled to maintain student interest during whole group instruction. Grade-level basals, the district mandate, were the only weapons these teacher warriors possessed because classroom libraries were scarce. Many teachers felt that their only recourse was to transfer out of the school, which meant a long line of first-year and new teachers came and left.

Arriving on this sad school scene was REA (Reading Excellence Act), with a determination to do the right things, with the right people, in the right way to improve student achievement. REA began by involving the staff in facing the music by using data to define the problems and determine the priorities. To be sure, it was hard to come to grips with the multifaceted problems and overwhelming challenges the staff had to face. Less than 40% of the children read on grade level and 80% of the students came from homes of poverty, many for which English was a second language.

Partnering with a university, REA worked with the school principal, literacy coach, and reading teacher to design an ambitious two-year plan of action. This plan of action was based on goals that grew out of student achievement data and data from classroom observations that portrayed current instructional practices. This data revealed that teachers relied predominately on whole-class instruction. Also, teacher-controlled instructional practices did not actively engage students in reading, writing, and talking about literature. Moreover, evidence of high-level text comprehension did not exist. When the staff talked about the data, one teacher observed, "Oh no—the longer some students stay here, the worse they perform." This marked a watershed moment for the school as staff members determined to change what they taught and how they taught.

In the quest for change, the leadership team planned and implemented varied job-embedded, professional development experiences. On Tuesdays, before school, the team invited teachers to join a book club in which they selected, read, and discussed various professional books. Once a month, teachers at each grade level got together with a university faculty member and the principal to study lesson plans. Teachers collaboratively developed lesson plans based on student needs and best practices in literacy. They implemented the lesson plans, reflected upon the lesson plans, and collected samples of student work that resulted from implementation. As the teams reviewed their reflections on their lessons and student work, they gained important insights about instruction. Gradually instruction became less teacher controlled and more student scaffolded. The literacy coach organized newly acquired, leveled nonfiction and fiction text sets in a book room for easy access and check-out. This act encouraged teachers to initiate small group instruction using differentiated materials.

REA was pleased with the two-year double-digit gains in student reading performance, and the staff continues to learn happily-ever-after in their professional learning community.

Sounds like a fairy tale? Well, it's not. This scenario is based on our long-term experiences in two schools that grew through change, increased student reading performance, and created supportive learning communities that nurtured strong, positive school cultures. We believe that this same scenario may be recreated in many, diverse settings, if there is an honest commitment to improvement. By shaping professional learning communities for literacy, school staffs can gain a renewed sense of efficacy about what they teach, how they teach, and what students learn.

WHAT ARE PROFESSIONAL LEARNING COMMUNITIES FOR LITERACY?

Schools that are professional learning communities for literacy succeed in improving practice and beat the odds by putting children first and believing that all children can succeed in reading (Taylor & Pearson, 2002). Professional learning communities share certain defining characteristics that educational researchers consider to be the best practices for leading school reform. When teachers, administrators, and others work together as professional learning communities to improve literacy, they

- Establish and contribute to collaborative, instructional teams that focus on improving literacy

- Clarify essential literacy outcomes that specify strategies, skills, and concepts that all students must learn for each semester and grade

- Develop in collaborative, instructional teams, formative common assessments to measure student learning of specific essential outcomes

- Establish a target score or benchmark for the common assessments to set high expectations and promote achievement among all students

- Administer the common assessments to all students at a given grade level

- Identify students who (1) did not meet the target, (2) met the target, and (3) exceeded the target on the common assessments

- Identify strengths and needs and generate strategies for improving teaching and learning

- Implement improvement strategies and support team members' efforts

- Assess the impact of collective efforts and continue gathering new data (Eaker, DuFour, & DuFour, 2002)

Professional learning communities for literacy evolve when teachers and administrators identify reading as a priority focus for school improvement and collaboratively share in decision making and problem solving. Their shared focus and collaborative ownership of achievement problems serve as the driving force for improvement. Moreover, professional learning communities for literacy determine the focus of their work by collecting and analyzing data about student achievement and classroom instructional practices.

WHY SHOULD WE COLLECT DATA ABOUT CURRENT LITERACY PRACTICES?

"Educational change depends on what teachers do and think. It's as simple and as complex as that" (Saranson as cited in Fullan & Stieglebauer, 1991, p. 117).

A first step for improving literacy is to move beyond a singular focus on what is taught. Improving literacy requires a reflective process that compares current literacy practices to research-based literacy practices. By gathering information about current teaching, the practices of colleagues can be scrutinized and compared to research-based pedagogy. Teaching tends to be an isolated profession with closed classroom doors that deter a natural sharing of practices and

118 THE LEARNING
COMMUNITIES
GUIDE TO
IMPROVING
READING
INSTRUCTION

knowledge among colleagues. Adult learners do not want to look bad in front of their peers and are threatened by the idea that colleagues may observe them and they will not be perfect. Yet it is important for teacher teams to reflect upon what they teach and how they teach to seek improvement. School improvement efforts succeed when professional development addresses the gap between the vision of research-based practice and the reality of current teaching practices. Effective leadership teams assist teachers in a nonthreatening way in gathering data on their classroom practices and reflecting upon that data.

WHAT SHOULD WE LOOK FOR WHEN EXAMINING CURRENT LITERACY PRACTICES?

"If we are going to call ourselves professionals, we are obligated to use best practices. Anything less is unacceptable" (DuFour, 2003, p. 71). When a consortium of superintendents asked us for a list of best practices that identified what principals should look for in classroom reading instruction, we searched for an existing observation tool. What we found was the *School Change Classroom Observation Scheme* developed at the Center for the Improvement of Early Reading Achievement (CIERA) under the leadership of Barbara Taylor and David Pearson (2000). We introduced CIERA's observation scheme as one possibility for gathering data on current teaching practices to a focus group of principals, reading specialists, teachers, and professional developers. The group's discussion of the components of CIERA's observation scheme inspired a deeper understanding of evidence-based literacy practices. Rather than adopting an observation scheme used for research purposes, we decided to tailor a flexible tool to guide teacher self-reflection on current teaching practices and schoolwide change in literacy.

What evolved was the Reading Reflection Survey, which engages teacher teams in thoughtful reflection about their literacy practices and links professional growth to student achievement. The primary purpose of the survey is to guide teachers in conversations about their classroom practices so they can establish goals for improvement.

The survey can be used in varied ways and for different purposes:

- As a friendly observer tool in classroom walk-throughs and peer coaching

- As a self-reflection tool for professional growth

- As a needs-assessment tool for planning professional development

- As a tool for lesson planning and lesson study

Peer coaches, mentors, school leadership teams, or outside observers such as university staff may choose to use the survey to observe in classrooms and look for evidence of research-based practices. Sometimes, however, teachers are not used to external observers, and observations may be too intimidating. In these schools, leadership teams may choose to use the survey as a self-reflection that fosters consideration of and conversation about research-based practices in reading. Also staff can reflect about research-based practices prior to conducting classroom observations. In this way, the staff becomes more familiar with the contents of the survey so that observations may be less intimidating.

To summarize, the survey helps identify professional development goals that reflect staff strengths and needs. Furthermore, the survey focuses conversations around five questions: (1) How is instruction personalized? (2) How does the environment facilitate learning? (3) How are students engaged? (4) What does the teacher do before, during, and after reading? and (5) What is the focus of teaching and learning? Each is described in Chapters 2–6 and reviewed in the following section.

How Is Instruction Personalized?

Personalizing instruction emphasizes the foremost element of successful teaching and learning—getting to know students. Personalizing instruction begins with assessing student interests, strengths, and needs and promotes opportunities for student choices. When reflecting on instructional practices, teachers consider the degree to which they differentiate instruction and match materials to student interests and needs.

How Does the Environment Facilitate Learning?

An environment that nurtures literacy fosters collaboration, communication, respect, and risk-taking—a learning community. This environment includes varied and flexible grouping options to engage students in reading, writing, and talking about literature. The section on grouping contains small group, whole group, paired, and independent or individual options. Small group instruction highlights two types: differentiated grouping such as guided reading, and small cooperative grouping, such as book clubs. Individual options consist of tutoring and independent work such as self-selected reading. Collaborative teaching is an inclusive grouping option where special teachers may work in the classroom to address the needs of gifted, Title I, or ESL students or students with disabilities while the classroom teacher is working with another group of students. Centers are considered an engaging grouping option as students work with classmates to complete literacy tasks independently while the teacher provides small group instruction.

To promote active student engagement, teachers increase small group, paired, and individual instruction and decrease whole group instruction. Whole group instruction is most appropriate when teachers model comprehension strategies, conduct shared reading, or read aloud to students. In spite of what research recommends, whole group instruction prevails. The survey encourages teacher teams to reflect upon their current grouping practices and to consider decreasing whole group instruction and differentiate instruction for diverse learners.

120 THE LEARNING
COMMUNITIES
GUIDE TO
IMPROVING
READING
INSTRUCTION

Effective literacy environments feature a wide variety of materials to engage students and personalize instruction. Exemplary reading instruction relies on rich literature that inspires students' writing and higher level talk about text. Exemplary teachers offer a wide variety of fiction and nonfiction reading materials to students. Age-appropriate, ability-level, and easy reading materials enable students to develop fluency. Leveled texts on gradient levels of difficulty are often used for guided reading instruction. Blown-up text may include transparencies of poems or other short passages, charts, or big books. Other types of texts found in classrooms that promote reading include student-teacher published work such as class books, word walls, student work displays, and reference charts such as rubrics or instructional posters.

How Are Students Engaged?

Exemplary teachers actively engage students in substantive tasks for reading, writing, and talking. These tasks involve students in using games, puzzles, manipulatives, instructional aids, computers, and journals. Worksheets and workbooks do not incorporate authentic reading of connected text; therefore prevalent use of these materials is discouraged.

The behaviors listed for student engagement primarily target whether students are actively engaged in reading, writing, or talking about text. When observing classrooms, it is desirable to find a high degree of active student engagement and a low frequency of passive student engagement. For the majority of instructional time, students should engage in reading, writing and talking about literature, rather than listening, oral turn taking, or round robin reading. Also, manipulating is another form of active student engagement and includes word games, dry erase boards, vocabulary cards, magnetic letters, and so on, that help students build vocabulary or word recognition skills. Finally, to promote independence and self-directed learning, the survey includes student self-assessment and verbalizing use of comprehension strategies.

What Does the Teacher Do
Before, During, and After Reading?

This section of the survey focuses on what the teacher does to guide students in the before reading, during reading, and after reading phases of instruction. When examining teacher behaviors, the preference is to observe student-scaffolded instruction as a predominant practice because that style is linked to reading achievement. Student-scaffolded practices include assessing, modeling, explaining, thinking aloud, coaching, scaffolding, and reading aloud. Additionally, we want to observe teachers using an elevated frequency of higher level questioning to promote deep understanding of text.

Teacher-controlled actions such as telling or low-level, interrogation-style questioning are often observed but are not associated with exemplary teaching and high achievement. These behaviors are included in italics on the Reading Reflection Survey to call attention to these two practices so teachers may consider decreasing frequency of use.

What Is the Focus of Teaching and Learning?

The fifth section of the Reading Reflection Survey, targets the "what," or content, of reading instruction. A balanced literacy program promotes teaching word study, vocabulary, fluency, and comprehension in the context of authentic reading. Word study components listed in the survey include letter identification, phonemic awareness, phonics, sight words, and word recognition strategies. Note that the survey delineates seven comprehension strategies described in Chapter 6. Comprehension instruction is grounded in authentic literature and includes text-explicit comprehension, or lower level thinking, and text-implicit comprehension, or higher order thinking. Higher order comprehension is fostered as students practice or apply comprehension strategies within authentic text rather than worksheets. The survey highlights the importance of students reading connected text, writing about text, and engaging in discourse about text. When students read connected text they read authentic materials such as trade books, magazines, and basal anthologies, rather than three- or four-paragraph passages on a worksheet.

Summary of Student and Teacher Engagement

Finally, observers or teacher teams are asked to reflect on the extent to which students are engaged in literacy activities. To judge the extent of engagement or time on task, observers or teachers consider the frequency with which students are engaged in reading, writing, and talking about text according to *rarely, occasionally, often,* and *usually* (the first column is used only for observation purposes). In summarizing teacher behaviors, consider the extent to which teachers model, coach, and engage in other student-scaffolded interactions.

To summarize, the Reading Reflection Survey (Figure 7.1) highlights the "look fors" of exemplary reading instruction. Also included are less effective behaviors and materials that are frequently observed in classrooms but are not linked to gains in student achievement. Relevant, instructional behaviors for literacy are organized under five categories: personalizing reading instruction, managing environments for literacy, ensuring student engagement, emphasizing active teaching, and targeting comprehension. The five categories of the survey provide a manageable and realistic focus for teacher teams and school leaders. Consideration and integration of all five components are necessary to

122 THE LEARNING
COMMUNITIES
GUIDE TO
IMPROVING
READING
INSTRUCTION

Figure 7.1   Reading Reflection Survey

READING REFLECTION SURVEY					
HOW IS INSTRUCTION PERSONALIZED?	**Observed**	**Rarely**	**Occasionally**	**Often**	**Usually**
1. Selects appropriate text for individual, small and whole group instruction					
2. Determines student interest, strengths, and needs					
3. Provides opportunities for choice					
4. Differentiates instruction in small groups					
5. Other					
HOW DOES THE ENVIRONMENT FACILITATE LEARNING?	**Observed**	**Rarely**	**Occasionally**	**Often**	**Usually**
6. Nurtures a classroom learning community that fosters collaboration, communication, respect, and risk taking					
7. Provides differentiated guided reading groups					
8. Organizes small group work in flexible, collaborative, book club groups					
9. Conducts whole class instruction in shared reading, mini-lessons, etc.					
10. Pairs students for buddy reading, writing, and word work					
11. Provides individual tutoring, instruction, or assessment					
12. Incorporates independent practice, reading, and writing					
13. Engages in collaborative teaching (special education, specialist)					
14. Establishes routines for productive student work					

READING REFLECTION SURVEY

HOW DOES THE ENVIRONMENT FACILITATE LEARNING?	Observed	Rarely	Occasionally	Often	Usually
15. Organizes and manages routines and literacy centers					
16. Schedules large blocks of time for reading, writing, and talking about text					
17. Emphasizes expanding tradebook collection— both fiction and nonfiction					
18. Uses leveled text sets					
19. Includes blown-up texts such as big books, transparencies, and charts					
20. Includes basal texts or anthologies					
21. Capitalizes on content textbooks					
22. Contains journals					
23. Features student and teacher published work					
24. Includes games, puzzles, and manipulatives					
25. Features an evolving word walls					
26. Minimizes use of worksheets and workbooks					
27. Incorporates computers and technology					
28. Emphasizes student work for modeling, reflecting, and assessing					
29. Features reference charts					
30. Other					
HOW ARE STUDENTS ENGAGED?	Observed	Rarely	Occasionally	Often	Usually
31. Reads connected texts (independent, paired, guided)					
32. Writes in response to reading text					

(Continued)

⊙ **Figure** 7.1 (Continued)

READING REFLECTION SURVEY

HOW ARE STUDENTS ENGAGED?	Observed	Rarely	Occasionally	Often	Usually
33. Manipulates literacy materials such as word cards or dry erase boards					
34. Talks about text in student-led small group discussions					
35. Verbalizes use of a comprehension strategy					
36. Responds orally in whole class dialogue					
37. Reflects and self-assesses					
38. Uses technology for word processing or practice					
39. Listens passively to teacher talk infrequently					
40. Other					
WHAT DOES THE TEACHER DO BEFORE, DURING AND AFTER READING?	**Observed**	**Rarely**	**Occasionally**	**Often**	**Usually**
41. Provides support *before* reading: introducing text, activating prior knowledge, and building background					
42. Supports readers *during* reading or guided reading phase					
43. Promotes comprehension *after* reading					
44. Models and demonstrates strategies that good readers use and explains how/why to use					
45. Coaches and scaffolds strategy use by prompting, probing, and questioning					
46. Supports student-led talk about text					
47. Reads aloud daily from a variety of material					
48. Thinks aloud to explain and demonstrate comprehension strategies					

READING REFLECTION SURVEY					
WHAT DOES THE TEACHER DO BEFORE, DURING, AND AFTER READING?	**Observed**	**Rarely**	**Occasionally**	**Often**	**Usually**
49. Assesses and records individual performance					
50. Observes, listens, and gives feedback					
51. Guides independent reading and writing practice in authentic texts					
52. Facilitates discussion using high-level questions to promote deep thinking					
53. Extends reading with drama, writing, rereading for fluency, etc.					
54. Limits the amount of teacher talk or telling					
55. Limits the use of an interrogative style or asking a series of low-level questions to the whole class					
56. Limits the use of round-robin reading					
57. Other					
WHAT IS THE FOCUS OF TEACHING AND LEARNING?	**Observed**	**Rarely**	**Occasionally**	**Often**	**Usually**
58. Applies word work in real text: letter identification, phonemic awareness, phonics, sight words, word recognition, spelling, word recognition strategies					
59. Provides both direct and indirect vocabulary development using authentic text					
60. Promotes fluency through rereading, modeling, choral reading, taped reading, etc.					
61. Fosters higher order thinking through talking and writing about text					

(Continued)

126 THE LEARNING
COMMUNITIES
GUIDE TO
IMPROVING
READING
INSTRUCTION

◉ **Figure 7.1** (Continued)

READING REFLECTION SURVEY					
WHAT IS THE FOCUS OF TEACHING AND LEARNING?	**Observed**	**Rarely**	**Occasionally**	**Often**	**Usually**
62. Applies predicting in connected text					
63. Applies making connections: text to self, text to text, text to world					
64. Applies summarizing in text					
65. Applies visualization in text					
66. Applies questioning in text					
67. Applies inferencing in text					
68. Applies monitoring and clarifying in text					
66. Teaches comprehension skills such as sequencing in context of real text					
67. Promotes writing in response to reading connected text as a routine					
68. Fosters oral language and discourse to promote higher order thinking and talking about text					
69. Other					
SUMMARY OF STUDENT AND TEACHER ENGAGEMENT	**Not Sure**	**Rarely**	**Occasionally**	**Often**	**Usually**
70. To what extent are students on task and engaged in high levels of reading, writing, and talking about text?					
71. To what extent does the teacher model, coach, and actively scaffold student learning?					

COMMENTS:

create vibrant literacy classrooms where all students become proficient at reading, writing, and talking about literature.

HOW CAN THE READING REFLECTION SURVEY BE INTRODUCED TO TEACHERS?

In the best classrooms, students are engaged much of the time in reading and writing, with the teacher monitoring student progress and encouraging continuous improvement and growth and providing scaffolded instruction, in which the teacher notices when students are having difficulty and provides sufficient support so that students are able to make progress. Furthermore this skillful instruction is based on the exact strategies students need to work on (Taylor, Pressley, & Pearson, 2002, p. 366).

Based on our experience in using the survey, we recommend that literacy leaders discuss the survey and its contents with teachers before the leadership team or teacher teams use the survey in classroom observations or for self-reflection. We find it crucial to prepare teachers for using the survey. Preparatory learning experiences provide a context for using the survey and nurture a deeper understanding of what the various behaviors look like. Leadership teams may consider two processes that we found successful.

One approach to introducing the survey involves teachers and administrators in conducting classroom observations and provides hands-on experience with the survey. As mentioned earlier, we created the Reading Reflection Survey when asked to conduct an audit of classroom reading practices and observe classroom instruction in six school districts that belonged to a school-university partnership. Before scheduling the classroom observations, we invited the principal, the reading specialist, and a classroom teacher leader from each school to a one-day orientation and demonstration of the Reading Reflection Survey.

We introduced the survey and defined those components for which participants needed clarification and explanation. Then we organized teams to visit several elementary and middle school classrooms of teachers who volunteered their classrooms as laboratories for our teams to observe and try out the Reading Reflection Survey. Teams conducted an hour-long observation and then met for 45 minutes to process what they observed. The teams discussed observed best practices, what they had questions about, what they found intriguing, and what they would change about the survey.

The hands-on experience with the survey by teachers and principals whose classrooms we would observe in the next few months created a positive attitude and feeling of ownership toward the observation protocol. One teacher commented at the end of the day, "Are you done with us or can we get together and observe and talk about classroom teaching again?" These teachers taught us that the protocol for gathering data is a powerful tool for discussion and reflection on best practices. This procedure was successful and we recommend it as one way to introduce the survey.

A second effective strategy for introducing the survey follows a workshop approach. We conduct these workshops in rural, suburban, and urban settings for whole-school faculties of elementary and middle schools. These workshops average about two or three hours and involve teacher teams in reading, writing, and talking about best practices in literacy as we model active teaching strategies. Recommended procedures are as follows:

1. Ask teams to brainstorm on sticky notes the best practices they would look for when observing a literacy classroom prior to introducing the survey. Teachers work with a partner for about five minutes to brainstorm and write one idea per sticky note.

2 Before the workshop starts, create five posters with headings that correspond to each section of the survey: teacher engagement, student engagement, grouping, content, and materials. Post these on the walls around the room.

3. Ask teacher pairs to arrive at consensus on how they will sort and place their sticky notes according to the five headings. Allow time for pairs to go to the posters and place their sticky notes.

4. Summarize quickly what the teacher pairs brainstormed for each of the five headings. This process accesses and honors teachers' prior knowledge about exemplary literacy practices.

5. Group teachers in cooperative groups that jigsaw an article describing what exemplary teachers do. Ask each cooperative group to create an illustration of the key ideas in their section of the article. Provide time for each group to share their products and thinking.

6. Discuss the overlap between what teams brainstormed prior to reading the article and what they learned from the article about best practices.

7. Allow faculty to view a video of a teacher engaged in literacy instruction and note observed behaviors on the survey.

Only after completing the procedures outlined above do we ask teachers to use the survey to reflect on their teaching. To complete the survey, teachers indicate their perception of the extent to which practices are prevalent by marking *rarely, occasionally, often,* or *usually* for each item. Note the first column is not used for self-reflection purposes. If the survey is used as an observation tool to collect data about schoolwide practices, we make several assurances to teachers. We tell teachers that the purpose of the observation is to collect data that guides professional development goal setting. We assure teachers that individual data is not shared with others and is not a part of the formal evaluation process. Only combined cross-grade data and grade-level team data are shared schoolwide. We also provide individual classroom data to teachers upon request. We find teachers receptive to using the survey when the results benefit them individually and collectively and the information is shared confidentially.

HOW IS THE SURVEY USED IN CLASSROOM OBSERVATIONS AND FOR SELF-REFLECTION?

We used a modified version of the Reading Reflection Survey to observe in hundreds of classrooms, for multiple purposes: auditing reading instruction, gathering data for professional development action plans, establishing base-line data for grant project evaluations, and evaluating progress of programs with pre- and post-observations. Usually, principals organize schedules for thirty-minute observations during reading instruction time in most, if not all, classrooms in the school. If possible, we observe all classrooms at a grade level to gather data for individual teachers, as well as data for grade teams' use in creating professional development goals.

To record observations, we combine qualitative note taking with a quantitative system of marking observed behaviors and instructional practices. We begin with qualitative note taking, where we script our observations. Then we "check off" observed behaviors in the first column ("Observed") so we can quantify frequencies of behaviors across classrooms or across multiple observations of the same teacher. Figure 7.2 presents a five-minute example of a transcript from an observation in a third-grade classroom. The observer uses abbreviations for the words *teacher* (T) and *student* (S) to quickly capture observations.

Analyzing the sample transcript, we find that the major teaching actions observed in this example are explaining, modeling, and assessing. Students were observed engaged in reading and writing activities, and fiction and non-fiction texts are used. Grouping patterns observed were independent work, paired reading, and small group guided reading. Content focused on writing, reading connected text, and a comprehension strategy: connecting to self.

◉ Figure 7.2 Sample Transcript Using Abbreviations

10:00 One pair takes turns reading trade book; another pair reading nonfiction book on snakes; an individual reading Spanish language trade book; small group of 4 writing readers' theater script. 6 Ss - independent reading. T works with 5 students in guided reading; leveled little book. T does mini-lesson on making connections to self, "You make your own unique and personal connections, . . ." T tells Ss this is a strategy good readers use. Reads 1 paragraph & thinks aloud to model. Asks Ss to use Post-its to mark "something in your own life." Ss read next three pages of text independently. T observes & makes notes. T asks one student to read aloud, notes errors.

HOW ARE THE DATA SUMMARIZED?

Frequencies for each observed practice or behavior on the survey can be summarized in different ways: (1) by calculating the number or percentage of classrooms in which each behavior is observed across grade levels or school-wide and (2) by noting behaviors observed in the same teacher's classroom during multiple observations that span over time. In grade-level teams, teachers discuss whether the data on observed practices represent standard classroom practice. Teams also discuss whether unchecked practices or behaviors on the survey are indicative of standard practice.

To make this more concrete, let's look at sample survey behaviors observed in four classrooms (Figure 7.3). Reading connected text and writing were observed in three of the four (75%) classrooms. In one classroom, no students (0%) were observed reading during any of the five sweeps. Telling or giving information was observed in all four classrooms (100%), and modeling, explaining, and demonstrating were observed in only one classroom (25%).

If school leadership teams use the survey for self-reflection rather than observation, teachers in grade-level teams note practices they perceive are used prevalently and those that are infrequently practiced or not used at all. Using a piece of flip chart paper for each category on the survey to create a graphic organizer, teachers use sticky dots to note *rarely, occasionally, often,* or *usually* for each behavior or practice in the category, so that they can view commonalities among them. Figure 7.4 shows a sample chart of four teachers' responses to student engagement items. This chart reveals that teachers perceive they often or usually engage students in passive responses such as listening and turn taking. The chart also indicates that students are engaged occasionally in student-led discussions in the four classrooms and that students often verbalize use of comprehension strategies in only one classroom. In all four classrooms, teachers perceive that students occasionally write in response to text.

Figure 7.3   Sample Frequency Analysis in Four Classrooms

Sample Behaviors Observed	#1 Classroom	#2 Classroom	#3 Classroom	#4 Classroom	Total #
Reads connected text		√	√	√	3 or 75%
Writes in response to reading		√	√	√	3 or 75%
Models, explains, and demonstrates				√	1 or 25%
Tells or gives information	√	√	√	√	4 or 100%

◉ Figure 7.4   Sample Chart of Four Teachers' Responses to Student Engagement Items

Active Engagement	Rarely	Occasionally	Often	Usually
1. Reads connected texts (independent, paired, guided)	● ● ●	●		
2. Writes in response to reading text		● ● ●		
3. Manipulates literacy materials such as word cards or dry erase boards	● ●	●		●
4. Talks about text in student-led small group discussions				● ● ● ●
5. Verbalizes use of a comprehension strategy		●		● ● ●
6. Responds orally in whole class dialogue	● ●	● ●		
Passive Engagement				
7. Listens to teacher tell or give information	● ● ● ●			
8. Takes turns in round-robin reading	● ●	● ●		
9. Takes turns in whole-class questioning or checking worksheets	● ● ● ●			

HOW CAN THE SURVEY RESULTS BE USED TO PLAN PROFESSIONAL DEVELOPMENT?

After the data are explained to teachers and compared to evidence-based practices, teachers consider this information to establish individual and collective professional growth goals. Figure 7.5 presents a chart we use to facilitate discussion about professional growth goals. This chart involves teacher teams in doing a gap analysis of research-based instructional practices and current reading instruction as indicated by observations and/or self-reflections. The gap analysis facilitates reflection and goal setting for professional development. The chart has four columns that correlate to guiding questions for teacher reflection and decision making:

1. What does reading instruction that reflects the research on how children learn best look like or sound like?

2. What strengths and weaknesses do our classroom survey data reveal as compared to our vision for reading instruction?

Figure 7.5   Sample Collaborative Commitment for Professional Learning

Collaborative Commitment for Professional Learning			
Our vision of effective literacy classrooms (based on research)	**Classroom survey data: What does current teaching looks like?**	**Barriers**	**Our learning commitments and goals**
We see ourselves supporting student learning to a greater extent by effective modeling of comprehension.	Strength: Students in our classrooms often or usually read connected text. Weakness: • We use telling quite a bit, which places students in a passive learning mode. • Modeling was observed in only one classroom.	We aren't sure about how to model and what the difference is between telling and explaining and modeling. We need time to learn together.	We plan to learn about modeling by: • Viewing videos • Reading about modeling and comprehension • Watching demonstrations • Creating collaborative lesson plans • Coaching each other

3. What barriers exist that get in the way of providing reading instruction that reflects how children learn best?

4. What learning commitments can we make that address the gap between our grade level's vision and classroom survey data?

For example, after examining student achievement data, classroom survey data, and information about research-based practices, teams determine that collectively they would like to learn more about how to model comprehension strategies effectively. Figure 7.5 provides a sample of how third-grade teachers collectively identified one professional development goal. Keep in mind that teachers could have more than one collective goal and different individual goals.

Engaging teachers in identifying collective and individual professional development goals builds ownership. Individual goals are essential because a team of teachers may have varied learning needs. Just because teachers teach the same grade does not necessarily mean they are at the same point along a continuum of instructional expertise. At a given grade level, we find less experienced classroom teachers who need additional support in promoting active student engagement. These teachers need to increase the frequency with which students read, write, and talk about text—especially after teacher modeling of comprehension strategies. On the other hand, other teachers at the same grade level actively engage students more frequently but could refine their expertise by learning to work more effectively with guided reading groups. All four teachers will work on modeling of comprehension strategies but will have other professional growth goals as well, based on their individual needs. Just as important, identifying a collective professional goal helps build collaboration and instructional consistency. Also, this collective act is crucial to developing professional learning communities that nurture and support teachers' growth in practice.

HOW DO WE CREATE A SUPPORTIVE ENVIRONMENT FOR SCHOOL AND CLASSROOM CHANGE?

The best teachers weave a variety of teaching activities together in an infinitely complex and dynamic response to the flow of classroom life, and the best school leaders weave school conditions together in an infinitely complex and dynamic response to life in schools. It is more like orchestration than straightforward implementation. (Duffy & Hoffman, 2002, p. 376)

We have observed that the complexity of change cannot be overestimated, especially when it comes to literacy instruction. Reading instruction is at once mysterious and challenging and cannot be reduced to a prescribed recipe that all teachers follow to achieve similar results. Because students differ, school contexts differ, materials differ, and teacher backgrounds differ, the recipe approach to literacy instruction does not work.

Effective leaders honor the collective experience and wisdom of teachers and embrace sustained change as a complex endeavor. Changing classroom practices requires a personalized approach in each school and demands a high degree of concrete support. Teachers, like their students, are learners who require modeling, scaffolding, and coaching in order to grow through change. The zone of proximal development applies to all learners—old and young alike. Sensitive leaders of literacy recognize this fact and fashion conditions for change that support all the learners in a school community.

We have had the good fortune to work with many effective school leaders through our work at the College of William and Mary. We have observed school leaders in rural, suburban, and urban schools in several states and found that those leaders who brought about major improvements in literacy all fostered certain school conditions. Certain conditions link inextricably to professional development, forming a reciprocal relationship that is key to school and classroom improvement. Simply put, professional development shapes certain conditions for change, and certain conditions for change are necessary for effective professional development.

In our collaborative work with Richard DuFour, we stress the impact of context on change and learning. DuFour reiterated to principals this message:

> I have come to understand the most significant contribution a principal can make to developing others is creating an appropriate context for adult learning. It is context—the programs, procedures, beliefs, expectations, and habits that constitute the norm for a given school—that plays the largest role in determining whether professional development efforts will have an impact on that school. (DuFour, 2001, p. 14)

What is a school context or environment that nurtures and supports school change? Effective leaders who implement and sustain school improvement focus their efforts on (1) increased student achievement, (2) collective teacher efficacy, (3) supportive school context, (4) effective professional development, (5) concrete pressure and support, and (6) cohesive dynamic interactions. Each of these conditions is described in the following section and illustrated in Figure 7.6.

Link to Student Achievement

Instructional leaders who successfully implement change link improvement efforts to student achievement by engaging staffs in using data to determine the focus and impact of professional development. In one rural partnership of seven schools, we began the school improvement process by involving staffs in a "data dig" where grade teams dug through a variety of student reading assessments. We served as friendly observers and visited classrooms to identify instructional practices that teachers used. The data we collected allowed teacher teams to compare their teaching with research-based practices that increase student reading proficiency. Principal and teacher focus group interviews, teacher efficacy surveys, and questionnaires elicited additional data. The staffs at each of the schools examined the data to identify priorities and professional development goals.

Acceptance of what the data suggest is sometimes difficult, and it takes diligent nudging by school leaders to bring reality into focus. One principal reflected,

> And I think that we had a long hard conversation because I think that we believed—and I probably believed to some degree, that they were doing much better than any test scores said, regardless of any documentation that we could produce. We all felt that we really don't have a huge problem. (Gregory, 2002, p. 101)

At another school, the staff initially denied the reliability of classroom observation results. These results suggested that small group instruction, modeling, scaffolding, and active learning strategies were not prevalent. The staff dug their heels in and assumed responsibility for change only after the principal confronted them by holding up the latest test scores and stating, "But these test results suggest that we need to change something to improve student performance. Couldn't this mean these observation results are accurate?"

◉ **Figure 7.6** Instructional Leadership for Change

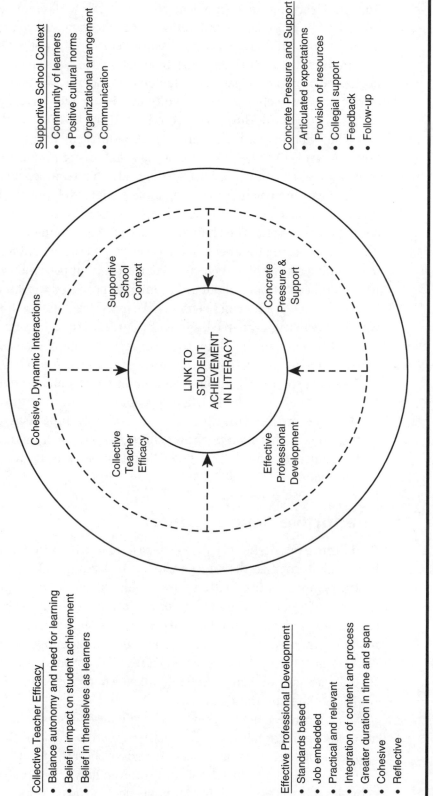

Cohesive, Dynamic Interactions
- Cohesiveness vs. fragmentation
- Recognition of relationships involved in change

Supportive School Context
- Community of learners
- Positive cultural norms
- Organizational arrangement
- Communication

Concrete Pressure and Support
- Articulated expectations
- Provision of resources
- Collegial support
- Feedback
- Follow-up

Collective Teacher Efficacy
- Balance autonomy and need for learning
- Belief in impact on student achievement
- Belief in themselves as learners

Effective Professional Development
- Standards based
- Job embedded
- Practical and relevant
- Integration of content and process
- Greater duration in time and span
- Cohesive
- Reflective

Within the diagram:

Cohesive, Dynamic Interactions

Supportive School Context

Collective Teacher Efficacy

LINK TO STUDENT ACHIEVEMENT IN LITERACY

Concrete Pressure & Support

Effective Professional Development

SOURCE: Gregory (2002)

136 THE LEARNING
COMMUNITIES
GUIDE TO
IMPROVING
READING
INSTRUCTION

Collective Teacher Efficacy

Instructional leaders recognize how teacher efficacy impacts change and improved learning. Teacher efficacy is a teacher's "judgment of his or her capabilities to bring out desired outcomes of student engagement and learning, even among those students who may be difficult or unmotivated" (Tschannen-Moran, Hoy, & Hoy, 2001, p. 783). Instructional leaders keep a focus on student needs and promote collective teacher efficacy, or "the perceptions of teachers in a school that the efforts of the faculty as a whole will have a positive effect on students" (Goddard, Hoy, & Woolfolk-Hoy, 2000, p. 479).

When working with a suburban REA-grant elementary school, we observed how powerful collective teacher efficacy is in moving a school toward improved teaching and learning. Specifically, the leadership team fostered teacher autonomy by involving teachers in setting professional development goals and inviting them to choose how they would achieve the goals from a variety of professional development options. The change in this staff was dramatic as they moved from not really believing they could increase literacy achievement among all students to becoming confident in their competence. For example, when we first began our work with a suburban school in Virginia, we projected the statement, "I believe our staff will leave no child behind." We asked teachers to "take a stand" as to whether they strongly agreed, agreed, disagreed, strongly disagreed, or were neutral with regards to this statement. Surprisingly, many didn't know what they believed, and a significant number either strongly disagreed or disagreed that the staff would leave no child behind and succeed in all children reading.

A couple of years later, when repeating the "human graph," there was a significant decrease in the number of staff who strongly disagreed or disagreed. At the heart of this change, the teachers began to trust themselves as learners and assumed responsibility and a take charge attitude to increase student achievement.

Supportive School Context

Effective instructional leaders shape a supportive school context for change. Principals recognize their responsibility in leading efforts to build a strong, positive school culture. Without a strong, positive school culture, teaching and learning will not improve. When principals model high expectations, nurture collegiality and caring, build trust, and encourage experimentation, they promote an environment conducive to learning and change. This environment is defined partially by twelve norms (Figure 7.7) associated with strong positive school cultures. Effective, school-embedded professional development is a vehicle for shaping these norms.

A supportive school context also eliminates barriers to learning by creating accommodating organizational structures, such as collaborative planning times, uninterrupted instructional schedules, and collaborative teaching. DuFour (2001) maintains, "In the right school context, even flawed professional development activities can serve as a catalyst for professional growth. Conversely, in the wrong school context, even programs with solid content and powerful training strategies are unlikely to be effective" (p. 14).

Figure 7.7 Norms for Strong Positive School Cultures

• Promote collegiality	• Encourage risk taking
• Set high expectations	• Build trust and confidence
• Provide tangible support	• Ground staff efforts in research
• Recognize accomplishments	• Respect, celebrate, and maintain humor
• Involve staff in decision making	• Protect priorities and values
• Honor and create traditions of professional learning communities	• Promote honest, open communication

SOURCE: Adapted from Saphier & King, 1985, p. 67

Effective Professional Development

Our work and our passion is leadership development of teachers, principals, and other administrators. A critical responsibility of leaders is modeling an intense love of learning. As the lead learners of the school, leadership team members build a shared value for professional development and continuous learning in their schools. Effective professional development ties teacher and administrator learning to student learning and occurs in the school.

School-based professional development embraces job-embedded forms such as lesson study, peer observations, action research, curriculum development, and assessment development. These types of professional development engage teachers in learning experiences that directly apply to their classrooms. Teacher change happens when professional development is relevant, practical, based on student needs, and allows for some teacher autonomy. Effective instructional leaders plan and implement professional development experiences that are cohesive, span over time, are of long duration, and respect the individual needs of teachers.

One Midwestern principal shared what she viewed as an important aspect of instructional leadership:

> If teachers see a need—but sometimes it is my job to help teachers see a need. Staff development evolves out of the school improvement plan. We plan next steps—they flow out of the plan. We match professional development and need—I insist on going back to the research. So I just plant the seeds because it won't work unless it comes from them. (Gregory, 2002, p. 99)

Concrete Pressure and Support

Teachers tell us that they are more encouraged to change instructional practices when leaders provide concrete pressure and support. The synergistic relationship between pressure and support moves teachers forward in trying new literacy practices. For change to occur, leaders must explicitly communicate their expectation that teachers will attempt or apply newly learned skills and concepts in the classroom. When leaders monitor teacher attempts and provide opportunities for teachers to discuss their attempts with colleagues, they support transfer of skills to the classroom.

Provision of resources supports teachers' implementation of new content and strategies learned through professional development. Specifically, teachers need time, team work, modeling, materials, supportive actions, monitoring, and follow-up. Over and over teachers say to us, "Don't expect us to make these great changes on our own—we need support, help, and materials."

What are some tangible ways that instructional leaders provide concrete pressure and support? One way is for leaders to change the schedule to create a longer, uninterrupted language arts block. This sends the message that reading is a priority. Second, "pushing in" Title I teachers and aides rather than pulling out students from the classroom supports differentiated, small group instruction. Moreover, this inclusive practice honors the uninterrupted language arts block. One administrator observed, "This change helped to meet the needs of children *and* teachers." Additionally, acquiring adequate materials and organizing a literacy library support small group reading instruction and independent, self-selected reading. Teachers said, "We know where every child is and we can match instruction to that level." Administrators agreed that "bringing in materials that the school did not have and showing teachers how to use leveled materials were key factors in improving reading. Last year we had very few books in the school and in classrooms; and that has increased dramatically."

Effective instructional leaders also provide concrete support by making time for job-embedded professional development. Effective instructional leaders make time in a variety of ways. Several principals banked time on a daily basis by shortening lunch time, increasing the school day, or diminishing transition times. By banking a certain number of minutes daily, these principals released students one afternoon a month to allow for professional development. Other administrators scheduled collaborative planning times during which they work with grade-level teams once or twice a month on targeted improvement efforts. The National Staff Development Council maintains that time for professional learning serves student learning and suggests the following strategies for creating blocks of time:

- Extending the school day

- Adding days to the school calendar

- Increasing the flexibility of educators' daily schedules

- Creating double planning periods

- Combining planning periods with other noninstructional time, such as lunch

- Combining classes for special subjects to allow some teachers to be released for professional development while others work with combined classes

- Reducing teacher administrative assignments (bus duty, lunch duty) and using the time for professional development

- Hiring subs to cover classrooms for an entire day, every other week, rotating them from classroom to classroom

- Limiting faculty meetings to one day a month so that study groups and so on meet the remaining days

- Scheduling four full days of content area classes and the fifth day for resource classes where students rotate to classes in music, art, computer lab, physical education, library, and science lab while classroom teachers spend the full day in professional development (Darling-Hammond, 1999; Murphy & Lick, 2001; Richardson, 2002).

Principals communicate the importance of learning when time is reserved on an ongoing basis for teacher teams to perfect their craft. When professional development is valued as a necessary and integral part of school improvement, leaders find ways to overcome time barriers.

> The logic for providing additional time for teachers to plan lessons together, review student work, analyze data, and find ways to assist low-performing students in meeting standards seems straightforward and compelling. And while making such changes may not be easy and requires navigating substantial barriers, it is eminently doable as the many schools that have already done it indicate. (Sparks, 2001, p. 2)

Cohesive, Dynamic Interactions

Finally, effective instructional leaders recognize that none of these conditions stands alone. All conditions are nested to create cohesive, dynamic interactions for improving teaching and learning. That is to say, sustained schoolwide change is facilitated by the dynamic interaction of a focus on student literacy, collective teacher efficacy, a supportive school context, effective professional development, and concrete pressure and support. For example, professional development that is not based on research will probably do little to improve literacy in schools. Likewise, if relationships are not considered in the professional development process so that collegiality is nurtured, teachers will be denied an important element of support, thereby decreasing the likelihood of change in classroom practices.

Partnerships With Parents

As a last word on leadership, recent research confirms something we have always known—parents make a difference (Taylor and Pearson, 2002). Effective school leaders form strong partnerships that improve teaching and learning. Parent partnerships are established when parents trust that the school has a strong concern for the welfare and learning of their children, not by superficial activities. When parents see evidence that the staff is working hard to improve learning, they become more active partners, providing varied kinds of support. To build parent partnerships, effective schools

140 THE LEARNING
COMMUNITIES
GUIDE TO
IMPROVING
READING
INSTRUCTION

- Invite parents to visit the school and their child's classroom

- Greet parents and students in the morning and afternoon

- Ask parents to attend "snack and chat" sessions with teachers at lunch time

- Provide child care during parent-teacher conferences

- Offer ongoing classes to parents about how they can help their children improve in reading and writing

- Give parents opportunities to volunteer to assist with the literacy program in a variety of ways

- Reduce communication barriers by having office staff who can communicate in the language of ESL parents

- Prepare parent-written communication using the native language of parents

- Establish parent centers that provide a place for parents to meet, work, and attend classes (Johnson, 2002)

WHAT TYPES OF SCHOOL-BASED PROFESSIONAL DEVELOPMENT WORK?

Traditionally, we have relied mainly on workshops for professional development. New research calls for more job-embedded models of professional development such as individually guided professional development, inquiry or action research, involvement in an improvement process, and observation/coaching (Sparks & Loucks-Horsely, 1990). Moreover, effective professional development that results in transfer to classroom practices

- Is of longer duration and spans over time

- Links staff learning to student learning

- Integrates curricular core content with instructional practices

- Promotes active learning among teachers

- Targets research-based practices

- Reduces fragmentation and is cohesive, connected, and systematic (Birman, Desimone, Porter, & Garet, 2000; Garet et al., 2001; National Staff Development Council, 2001).

In addition, how teachers receive professional development and follow-up support impacts whether they transfer what they learn to classroom practice. Transfer of professional development to classroom practice is greatest when whole-school faculties participate in professional development followed by peer coaching teams. Figure 7.8 summarizes findings about patterns of participation in professional development and levels of implementation (Joyce & Showers, 1995).

Figure 7.8 Pattern of Participation in Professional Development and Level of Implementation

Pattern of Participation	Level of Implementation
• No peer structure for follow-up • Participation by individual volunteers	5–10% implementation
• Peer coaching teams • Participation from a variety of schools	75% implementation
• Peer coaching teams • Participation by whole-school faculties	90% or better—can reach 100%

Job-embedded professional development includes a variety of types such as individually guided professional development, inquiry or action research, involvement in an improvement process, and observation/coaching. Job-embedded professional development is effective because it builds "a framework of shared responsibility" (Conzemius & O'Neill, 2001, p. 11). This framework includes three elements that shape professional learning communities:

- *Focus:* creates shared clarity of thought, direction, and purpose

- *Reflection*: helps people learn from what they've done in the past and identify better ways of accomplishing their goals

- *Collaboration:* brings people together to share ideas and knowledge (Conzemius & O'Neill, 2001, p. 11).

Study groups, an inquiry-based model of professional development, reflect characteristics of effective professional development and integrate focus, reflection, and collaboration. Study groups are particularly cost-effective and influential in changing classroom practice.

A professional study group is a small number of individuals who engage in focused inquiry that increases their capacity to improve student learning (Murphy & Lick, 2001). This group may meet before or after school, during early release of students, during common planning time, or during the day when roving substitutes cover classes. When teachers participate in a study group, they learn about the latest research on reading and become familiar with exemplary children's literature. Moreover, study groups honor teacher needs and backgrounds while providing a nonthreatening learning environment for attempting new instructional practices and receiving feedback (Robb, 2000b). The following are guiding principles for study groups. Effective study groups

- Focus on research-based strategies to improve teaching and learning

- Include teachers from across the grade levels

- Are student centered and based on achievement data

- Develop an action plan for operating that evolves from SMART goals (Conzemius & O'Neill, 2001)

- Are supported internally by literacy coaches

- Are lead by external facilitators who provide modeling, coaching, and scaffolding

- Meet at least once a month, over four or five months

- Include opportunities for the entire school faculty involvement

- Focus inquiry on the question, "What are students learning and achieving as a result of what teachers are learning and doing in study groups?" (Murphy & Lick, 2001, p. 12)

- Share leadership among group members

- Create publicly shared products such as video tapes, student work, and lesson plans (Murphy & Lick, 2001; Taylor, 2003)

Let's examine one study group in practice to get a feel for how an effective study group operates. This particular study group started with third- and fourth-grade teachers with a similar interest in modeling high-level comprehension. The teacher teams began by identifying a SMART goal. SMART goals are *specific* and *strategic*, *measurable*, *achievable*, *results-driven*, and *time-bound* (Conzemius & O'Neill, 2001, pp. 89–90). Figure 7.9 provides a sample SMART goal and explains why the goal is SMART.

◉ Figure 7.9   Sample SMART Goal and Explanation

SMART GOAL: In two years at least 70% of all third-, fourth-, and fifth-grade students will pass the comprehension subtest on the state assessment.	
Specific and strategic	This goal is specific and strategic because it focuses on students in Grades 3, 4, and 5 and targets reading comprehension, the greatest area of need.
Measurable	This goal is measurable because the state standardized test score provides this information on a yearly basis.
Achievable	This goal is achievable because currently 40% of all third-, fourth-, and fifth-grade students are passing the comprehension subtest on the state assessment. This goal is not too easy or too difficult—it is just right.
Results-driven	This goal is results-driven because it states, "70% of all third-, fourth-, and fifth-grade students will pass the comprehension subtest . . . " This goal does not focus on what teachers will do to achieve the outcome.
Time-bound	This goal is time-bound because it identifies a specific deadline for achieving the goal—two years.

Figure 7.10   Sample Study Group Action Plan

Actions	Resources	Products	Number of Group Meetings	Teacher/Student Evidence
Read literature about comprehension strategies	IRA materials and journals *Strategies that Work*	Classroom posters, charts, bookmarks on comprehension strategies	All meetings	Teacher reflection journals
Do think alouds to model comprehension strategies in whole group or small group instruction	Videos on think alouds Fiction and nonfiction literature	Collaborative lesson plans using literature and comprehension strategies	Seven meetings (one strategy per meeting)	Reader response options Observations Teacher reflection journals
Increase time allotted for student reading and writing for high-level comprehension.	Easy materials for independent reading	Journal of written observations and reflections, reading time, and strategy use	Ongoing throughout study group operation	Student reading logs Student reflections about strategy use Teacher reflection journals
Videotape each member of the study group modeling and thinking aloud a comprehension strategy	Video recorder	Videotapes of teachers	Ongoing and periodical	Reader response options Observations Teacher reflection journals

After establishing the SMART goal, the study group created an action plan for how they would achieve the goal. The group based their action plan on what they read about effective practices for teaching comprehension. Figure 7.10 provides a sample action plan the study group created. This group plans to meet twice a month, for almost five months. During this time, they plan to read, apply study group content in their classrooms, examine student evidence, discuss, and reflect on how things are going. They also plan to view each other's videotapes and provide feedback for reflection.

When the group implements their plan, they follow an agenda and adopt certain roles for each meeting (Taylor, 2003). Group members decide on study group roles, and one person agrees to serve as facilitator. Group roles rotate from one meeting to the next and may include a facilitator, a recorder who keeps the study group meeting notes, a time keeper, a task master, an encourager, and so on. Study group meetings usually last no more than an hour and follow a routine agenda that includes reflecting, discussing, shared learning, and planning. Figure 7.11 provides more in-depth information about these study group actions.

144 THE LEARNING
COMMUNITIES
GUIDE TO
IMPROVING
READING
INSTRUCTION

◉ Figure 7.11   Sample Study Group Agenda

Allotted Time	Action
10 minutes	***Reflecting*** • Use journal to reflect on actions since last meeting. • Share reflections with group in brief manner.
10 Minutes	***Discussing*** • Talk about article/book the group read since last meeting. OR • Review student work resulting from classroom actions since the last group meeting.
25–30 Minutes	***Shared Learning*** • Learn a new technique (i.e., watching a commercial video, engaging in a learning activity, observing a facilitator model). OR • View two group members' videos to reflect, provide feedback, and enhance teaching.
10–15 Minutes	***Planning*** • Determine what group members should accomplish prior to the next study group meeting. • Decide on what will be done at the next group meeting and member responsibilities for that meeting (roles, materials, etc.).

SOURCE: Taylor (2003)

During *shared learning*, the group alternates between learning a new technique or viewing two members' videos of their teaching. All group members learn a great deal by observing each other in practice. To achieve the greatest benefit from the video sharing, the group follows a procedure that includes viewing a 5–10 minute clip of a teacher teaching a part of a lesson. While viewing the video, group members think about how they will respond to these four guiding questions (Taylor, 2003):

1. What things were the students able to do relative to the study group focus? What things went well?

2. What was the teacher doing to help students be successful relative to the study group focus?

3. What else could the teacher have done to help students be successful relative to the study group topic?

4. What did you learn that will help you improve teaching and learning in your classroom?

At this point you may be thinking, "This sounds like a practical, relevant, and collaborative way to engage teachers in job-embedded, student-focused professional development. However, there have to be some pitfalls that keep study groups from being effective." Problems arise that affect study groups, and proactive planning avoids these problems. In particular, leaders are cautioned to avoid the following pitfalls:

- Not focusing on a research-based strategy

- Not sticking to a topic for a significant amount of time (3–5 months)

- Not looking at student-achievement and instructional data

- Sharing ideas or talking about kids, instead of working to improve instruction

- Spending study group time discussing problems or issues instead of focusing on actions (Taylor, 2003)

Creating an action plan is one deterrent to the described pitfalls. Also, maintaining study group meeting notes that are shared with leadership teams on a regular basis builds in a process for monitoring and supporting group progress. Many schools find it helpful to create a study group steering committee that meets monthly to discuss study group progress and problems. The study group steering committee is made up of the school administrators, an external facilitator, a literacy coach, and one member of each study group team. In summary, school leaders must connect teacher learning to student needs. If school leaders do not monitor student progress, plan appropriate professional development, and leverage necessary resources, then schools will not achieve or sustain high levels of learning for all students (Rozzelle, 1996).

WHAT WERE THE BIG IDEAS IN THIS CHAPTER?

This chapter describes how professional learning communities for literacy can be established and supported. Professional learning communities begin by using a wide array of data to focus improvement efforts for literacy. We built a case for collecting data about current instructional practices so that teacher teams can compare current practice to research-based literacy practices. This reflective process can be facilitated by using the Reading Reflection Survey. By using this survey, schools can target professional development goals that will link to student achievement. We also described the necessity for shaping supportive school environments that foster effective, job-embedded, professional development. Finally, we described professional development models emphasizing an inquiry-based model: study groups.

CONSTRUCTIVE REFLECTION

Process the big ideas in this chapter by using the Reading Reflection Survey presented in Figure 7.1. Teams may use the survey as a self-reflection tool for discussion or as a protocol for friendly observations of classrooms. In either case, reflect upon the results and use the graphic organizer that is presented in Figure 7.12 to establish team and personal goals for improving literacy instruction. Discuss strategies for achieving goals.

◉ Figure 7.12 Goal Setting for Literacy Instruction

Goal Setting for Literacy Instruction

(Use the Reading Reflection Survey [Figure 7.1] to identify goals for improving literacy in your classroom.)

Component of the Reading Observation & Reflection Survey	Goal	Actions to Take
Teacher Engagement		
Student Engagement		
Grouping		
Instructional Content		
Instructional Materials		

References

Adams, M. J. (1990). *Beginning to read.* Cambridge, MA: Harvard University Press.

Afflerbach, E. (1999). Teacher's choices in classroom assessment. In S. J. Barrentine (Ed.), *Reading assessment: Principles and practices for elementary teachers.* Newark, DE: International Reading Association.

Allen, J. (2002). *On the same page: Shared reading beyond the primary grades.* Portland, ME: Stenhouse.

Allen, J. (2003). *Words, words, words: Teaching vocabulary in grades 4–12.* Portland, ME: Stenhouse.

Allington, R. (2001). *What really matters for struggling readers: Designing research-based programs.* New York: Longman.

Allington, R. (2002). What I've learned about effective reading instruction from a decade of studying exemplary elementary classroom teachers. *Phi Delta Kappan, 83*(10), 740–747.

Allington, R. L., & Johnston, P. H. (Eds.). (2002). *Reading to learn: Lessons from exemplary fourth-grade classrooms.* New York: Guilford Press.

Allington, R., & McGill-Franzen, A. (2003). The impact of summer setback on the reading achievement gap. *Phi Delta Kappan, 85*(1), 68–75.

Armbruster, B., Lehr, F., and Osborn, J. (2001). *Put reading first: The research building blocks for teaching children to read, kindergarten through grade 3.* Ann Arbor, MI: Center for the Improvement of Early Reading Achievement (CIERA).

Baker, L. (2002). Metacognition in comprehension instruction. In C. C. Block & M. Pressley (Eds.), *Comprehension instruction: Research-based best practices* (pp. 85–88). New York: Guilford Press.

Baker, S., Simmons, D. and Kameenui, E. (1995). *Vocabulary acquisition: Synthesis of the research.* Technical Report No. 13. University of Oregon, National Center to Improve the Tools of Education.

Beck, I. L., & McKeown, M. G. (1991). Condition for vocabulary acquisition. In R. Barr, M. Kamil, P. Mosenthal, & P. D. Pearson (Eds.), *Handbook of reading research* (Vol. II, pp. 789–814). White Plains, NY: Longman.

Beck, I. L., & McKeown, M. G. (1999). Getting the discussion started. *Educational Leadership, 57*(3), 25–28.

Beers, K. (2003). *When kids can't read: What teachers can do.* Portsmouth, NH: Heinemann.

Bellanca, J., & Fogarty, R. (2001). *Blueprints for thinking in the cooperative classroom.* Arlington Heights, IL: Skylight Training and Publishing.

Birman, B. F., Desimone, L., Porter, A. C., & Garet, M. S. (2000). Designing professional development that works. *Educational Leadership, 57*(8), 28–33.

Blachowicz, C., & Ogle, D. (2001). *Reading comprehension: Strategies for independent learners.* New York: Guilford Press.

Block, C. C., Schaller, J. L., Joy, J. A., & Gaine, P. (2002). Process-based comprehension instruction: Perspectives of four reading educators. In C. C. Block & M. Pressley (Eds.), *Comprehension instruction: Research-based best practices* (pp. 42–61). New York: Guilford Press.

Brown, M. W. (1949). *The important book.* New York: Harper.

Bunting, E. (1997). *I am the mummy Heb-Nefert.* New York: Harcourt Brace.

Burke, K. (2000). *What to do with a kid who: Developing cooperation, self discipline and responsibility in the classroom.* Arlington Heights, IL: Skylight Training and Publishing.

Calkins, L. M. (2001). *The art of teaching reading.* New York: Longman.

Cassetta, G. (2001). *Literacy centers: A standards-based approach for grades 3 and beyond.* Wellington, NZ: Learning Media.

Center for Gifted Education. (1998). *Journeys and destinations.* Dubuque, IA: Kendall/Hunt.

Center for Gifted Education, College of William and Mary. (1998). *Literary reflections: A language arts unit for high-ability learners.* Dubuque, IA: Kendall/Hunt.

Center for Gifted Education. (1999). *Guide to teaching a language arts curriculum for high-ability learners.* Dubuque, IA: Kendall/Hunt.

Clay, M. M. (1993). *An observation survey of early literacy achievement.* Portsmouth, NH: Heinemann.

College Entrance Examination Board. (2003). *The neglected "R": The need for a writing revolution.* New York: College Entrance Examination Board.

Conzemius, A., & O'Neill, J. (2001). *Building shared responsibility for student learning.* Alexandria, VA: Association for Supervision and Curriculum Development.

Csikszentmihalyi, M. (1990). *Flow: The psychology of optimal experience.* New York: Harper Perennial.

Darling-Hammond, L. (1999). Target time toward teachers. *Journal of Staff Development, 20*(2), 31–36.

Dewey, J. (1913). *Interest and effort in education.* Boston: Riverside.

Dorn, L. J., & Soffos, C. (2001). *Scaffolding young writers: A writers' workshop approach.* Portland, ME: Stenhouse.

Dreikurs, R. (1971). *Social equality: The challenge of today.* Chicago: Henry Regnery Company.

Duffy, G. (2003). *Explaining reading: A resource for teaching concepts, skills, and strategies.* New York: Guildford Press.

Duffy, G. D., & Hoffman, J. V. (2002). Beating the odds in literacy education: Not the "betting on" but the "bettering of" schools and teachers? In B. M. Taylor & P. D. Pearson (Eds.), *Teaching reading: Effective schools, accomplished teachers.* Mahwah, NJ: Lawrence Erlbaum.

DuFour, R. (2001). In the right context. *Journal of Staff Development, 22,* 14–17.

DuFour, R. (2003). The leading edge. *Journal of Staff Development,* Spring.

Duke, N. (2003, July). *Comprehension difficulties.* Presented at the 2003 CIERA Summer Institute, Ann Arbor, MI.

Durkin, D. 1979. What classroom observations reveal about reading instruction. *Reading Research Quarterly, 14,* 481–533.

Eaker, R., DuFour, R., & DuFour, R. (2002). *Getting started: Reculturing schools to become professional learning communities.* Bloomington, IN: National Educational Service.

Fletcher, R., & Portalupi, J. (1998). *Craft lessons: Teaching writing K-8.* Portland, ME: Stenhouse.

Fletcher, R. (1996). *A writer's notebook: Unlocking the writer within you.* New York: Avon Books.

Flynt, E. S., & Cooter, R. B. (1999). *English-Espanol reading inventory for the classroom.* Upper Saddle River, NJ: Merrill/Prentice Hall.

Fogarty, R. (2001). *Teachers make THE difference.* Chicago: Fogarty.

Fogarty, R. (2002). *Brain compatible classrooms* (2nd ed.). Arlington Heights, IL: Skylight Professional Development.

Fountas, I. C., & Pinnell, G. S. (2001). *Guiding readers and writers grades 3–6: Teaching comprehension, genre, and content literacy.* Portsmouth, NH: Heinemann.

Fullan, M., & Stieglebauer, S. (1991). *The new meaning of educational change.* New York: Teachers College Press.

Gardner, H. (1983). *Frames of mind: The theory of multiple intelligences.* New York: Basic Books.

Garet, M., Porter, A. C., Desimone, L., Birman, B. F., and Suk Yoon, K. (2001). What makes professional development effective? Results from a national sample of teachers. *American Educational Research Journal, 38*(4) 915–945.

Glasser, W. (1986). *Control theory in the classroom.* New York: Harper and Row.

Goddard, R., Hoy, W. K., & Woolfolk-Hoy, A. (2000). Collective teacher efficacy: Its meaning, measure, and impact on student achievement. *American Educational Research Journal, 37,* 479–508.

Goodman, K. S. (1969). Analysis of reading miscues: Applied psycholinguistics. *Reading Research Quarterly, 5,* 9–13.

Gregory, V. (2002). *A study of professional development at three midwestern, urban, public, elementary schools with increased student achievement in language arts.* Unpublished dissertation, College of William and Mary, Williamsburg, VA.

Guthrie, J. T. (2004). *Classroom practices promoting engagement and achievement in comprehension.* Reno, NV: International Reading Association Research Conference.

Guthrie, J. T., VanMeter, P., Hancock, G. R., Alao, S., Anderson, E., & McCann, A. (1998). Does concept-oriented reading instruction increase strategy use and conceptual learning from text? *Journal of Educational Psychology, 90,* 261–278.

Harris, T. L., & Hodges, R. E. (1995). *The literacy dictionary: The vocabulary of reading and writing.* Newark, DE: International Reading Association.

Harste, J. C., Shorte, K. G., & Burke, C. (1996). *Creating classrooms for authors and inquirers.* Portsmouth, NH: Heinemann.

Harvey, S., & Goudvis, A. (2000). *Strategies that work: Teaching comprehension to enhance understanding.* Portland, ME: Stenhouse.

Hoffman, J. (2003). *Assessing the literacy environment of the elementary classroom.* Presented at the 2003 CIERA Summer Institute, Ann Arbor, MI.

Hopkins, L. B. (1994). *Hand in hand: An American history through poetry.* New York: Simon and Schuster.

Hoyt, L. (2000). *Snapshots: Literacy minilessons up close.* Portsmouth, NH: Heinnemann.

HuffBenkoski, K. A., & Greenwood, S. C. (1995). The use of word analogy instruction with developing readers. *The Reading Teacher, 48*(5), 446.

Ivey, G. (2002). Responsibility and respect for themselves and for whatever it is they're doing: Learning to be literate in an inclusive classroom. In R. L. Allington & P. H. Johnston (Eds.), *Reading to learn: Lessons from exemplary fourth-grade classrooms.* New York: Guilford Press.

Johnson, C. D. (2003, August). *Factors considered in leveling books.* Presented at The College of William and Mary Leadership and Literacy Academy, Williamsburg, VA.

Johnson, D., & Pearson, P. D. (1984). *Teaching reading vocabulary* (2nd ed.). New York: Holt, Rinehart & Winston.

Johnson, D. W., & Johnson, R. T. (1986). *Circles of learning: Cooperation in the classroom.* Alexandria, VA: Association of Supervision and Curriculum Development.

Johnson, J. F. (2002). High-performing, high-poverty, urban elementary schools. In B. M. Taylor & P. D. Pearson (Eds.), *Teaching reading: Effective schools, accomplished teachers.* Mahwah, NJ: Lawrence Erlbaum.

Joyce, B., & Showers, B. (1995). *Student achievement through staff development: Fundamentals of school renewal* (2nd ed.). White Plains, NY: Longman.

Juel, C., & Minden-Cupp, C. (2000). Learning to read words: Linguistic units and instructional strategies. *Reading Research Quarterly, 35,* 458–492.

Keene, E. O., & Zimmerman, S. (1997). *Mosaic of thought: Teaching comprehension in a reader's workshop.* Portsmouth, NH: Heinemann.

Kemp (1994). Word storm: Connecting vocabulary to the student's database. In T. Rasinski, N. D. Padak, B. W. Church, G. Fawcett, J. Hendershot, J. M. Henry, et al. (Eds.), *Teaching word recognition, spelling, and vocabulary: Strategies from the reading teacher.* Newark, DE: International Reading Association.

Klingner, J. K., & Vaughn, S. (1998). Using collaborative strategic reading. *Teaching Exceptional Children, July-August,* 32–37.

Koch, K. (1970). *Wishes, lies, and dreams: Teaching children to write poetry.* New York: Chelsea House.

Leslie, L., & Caldwell, J. (2001). *Qualitative Reading Inventory-3.* New York: Addison Wesley Longman.

Lyons, C. A. (2003). *Teaching struggling readers: How to use brain-based research to maximize learning.* Portsmouth, NH: Heinemann.

Moje, E. (2003, July). *Developing literacy in the content areas.* Presented at the 2003 CIERA Summer Institute, Ann Arbor, MI.

Morrow, L. M. (1997). *The literacy center: Contexts for reading and writing.* York, ME: Stenhouse.

Murphy, C. U., & Lick, D. (2001). *Whole-faculty study groups: Creating student-based professional development.* Thousand Oaks, CA: Corwin Press.

Nagel, G. (2001). Questions teachers are asking about grouping. *The California Reader, 35,* 31–35.

Nagy, W. E. (1988). *Teaching vocabulary to improve comprehension.* Newark, DE: International Reading Association.

Nagy, W., & Herman, P. (1987). Breadth and depth of vocabulary knowledge: Implications for acquisition and instruction. In M. McKeown & M. Curtis (Eds.), *The nature of vocabulary acquisition.* Hillsdale, NJ: Erlbaum.

National Reading Panel. (2000). *Teaching children to read: An evidence-based assessment of the scientific research literature on reading and its implications for reading instruction: Reports of the subgroups.* Washington, DC: National Institute of Child Health and Development.

National Staff Development Council. (2001). *Tools for growing the NSDC standards.* Oxford, OH: Author.

New Zealand Ministry of Education. (1997). *Reading for life: The learner as a reader.* Huntington Beach, CA: Pacific Learning.

Ohlhausen, M., & Jepson, M. (1992). Lessons from Goldilocks: "Somebody's been choosing my books but I can make my own choices now!" *The New Advocate, 5,* 31–46.

Palinscar, A. S., & Brown, A. L. (1984). Reciprocal teaching of comprehension: Fostering and monitoring activities. *Cognition and Instruction, 2,* 117–175.

Paris, S. G., Lipson, M. Y., & Wixson, K. K. (1983). Becoming a strategic reader. *Contemporary Educational Psychology, 8,* 293–316.

Pavelka, P. (2002). *Guided reading management: Structure and organization for the classroom: Grades 1–3.* East Lyme, CT: Husky Trail Press.

Pearson, P. D , Cervetti, G., & Jaynes, C. (2003, July). *Using research to guide professional development within the CIERA school-change project: The case of Patterson Elementary.* Presented at the 2003 CIERA Summer Institute, Ann Arbor, MI.

Pearson, P. D., Roehler, L. R., Dolle, J. A., & Duffy, G. G. (1992). Developing expertise in reading comprehension. In J. Samuels & A. Farstrup (Eds.), *What research has to say about reading instruction.* Newark, DE: International Reading Association.

Pressley, M. (1999). Self-regulated comprehension processing and its development through instruction. In L. B. Gambrell, L. M. Morrow, S. B. Neuman, & M. Pressley (Eds.), *Best practices in literacy instruction.* New York: Guilford Press.

Pressley, M. (2002). *Reading instruction that works: The case for balanced teaching.* New York: Guilford Press.

Pressley, M. (2003, July). *Balanced reading instruction.* Presented at the 2003 CIERA Summer Institute, Ann Arbor, MI.

Raphael, T. (2003, May). *Connected learning experiences.* Presented at the annual meeting of the International Reading Association, Orlando, FL.

Rasinski, T., Padak, N. D., Church, B. W., Fawcett, G., Hendershot, J., Henry, J. M., et al. (Eds.). (2000). *Teaching word recognition, spelling, and vocabulary: Strategies from the reading teacher.* Newark, DE: International Reading Association.

Ray, K. W. (1999). *Wondrous words: Writers and writing in the elementary classroom.* Urbana, IL: National Council of Teachers of English.

Reutzel, D. & Cooter, R. (1992). *Teaching children to read: From basals to books.* New York: Macmillan Publishing Company.

Rice, M. S. (2003, July). *Vocabulary and reading comprehension in the elementary and middle grades.* Presented at the 2003 CIERA Summer Institute, Ann Arbor, MI.

Richardson, J. (2002). Think outside the clock. In *Tools for schools.* Oxford, OH: National Staff Development Council.

Robb, L. (2000a). *Teaching reading in middle school.* New York: Scholastic.

Robb, L. (2000b). *Redefining staff development: A collaborative model for teachers and administrators.* Portsmouth, NH: Heinemann.

Robb, L. (2003). *Teaching reading in social studies, science, and math.* New York: Scholastic.

Routman, R. (2003). *Reading essentials.* Portsmouth, NH: Heinemann.

Rozzelle, J. (1996). *The long-term effectiveness of the Reading Recovery program.* Unpublished dissertation, College of William and Mary, Williamsburg, VA.

Saphier, J., & King, M. (1985). Good schools grow in strong cultures. *Educational Leadership, 38*(6), 66–77.

Sejnost, R., & Thiese, S. (2001). *Reading and writing across the content areas.* Arlington Heights, IL: SkyLight Training and Publishing.

Sparks, D. (2001). Time for professional learning serves student learning. *Results,* November, 2.

Sparks, D., & Loucks-Horsely, S. (1990). *Five models of staff development.* Oxford, OH: National Staff Development Council.

Stahl, S. (2001). Teaching phonics and phonological awareness. In S. B. Neuman & D. K. Dickinson (Eds.), *Handbook of early literacy research* (pp. 333–347). New York: Guilford Press.

Stahl, S. A., & Fairbanks, M. M. (1986). The effects of vocabulary instruction: A model-based meta-analysis. *Review of Educational Research, 56,* 72–110.

Stanovich, K.E. (1986). Matthew effects in reading: Some consequences of individual differences in the acquisition of literacy. *Reading Research Quarterly, 21*(4), 360–406.

Taylor, B. (2003, May). *Scaling up: Using the CIERA school change framework with 24 REA schools.* Presented at the annual meeting of the International Reading Association, Orlando, FL.

152 THE LEARNING
COMMUNITIES
GUIDE TO
IMPROVING
READING
INSTRUCTION

Taylor, B. M. (2003, July). *Leading faculty in productive study groups.* Presented at the Annual Summer Institute of CIERA, Ann Arbor, MI.

Taylor, B. M., & Pearson, P. D. (2000). *The CIERA school change classroom observation scheme.* Minneapolis, MN: Center for the Improvement of Early Reading Achievement.

Taylor, B.M., & Pearson, P. D. (Eds.) (2002). *Teaching reading: Effective schools, accomplished teachers.* Mahwah, NJ: Lawrence Erlbaum.

Taylor, B., Pressley, M., & Pearson, P. D. (2002). Research-supported characteristics of teachers and schools that promote reading achievement. In B. Taylor & P. D. Pearson (Eds.), *Teaching reading: Effective schools, accomplished teachers* . Mahwah, NJ: Lawrence Erlbaum.

Tovani, C. (2000). *I read it, but I don't get it: Comprehension strategies for adolescent readers.* Portland, ME: Stenhouse.

Tschannen-Moran, M., Hoy, W. K., & Hoy, A. W. (2001). Teacher efficacy: Capturing an illusive construct. *Teaching and Teacher Education, 17,* 783–805.

Vygotsky, L. (1978). *Mind in society: The development of higher psychological processes.* Cambridge, MA: Harvard University Press.

Wang, M. C., Haertel, G. D., & Walberg, H. J. (1993). Toward a knowledge base for school learning. *Review of Educational Research, 63*(3), 249–294.

Wilbur, R. (1956). *Things of this world.* New York: Harcourt Brace.

Williams, J. P. (2002). Using the theme scheme to improve comprehension. In C. C. Block & M. Pressley (Eds.), *Comprehension instruction: Research-based best practices* (pp. 126–139). New York: Guilford Press.

Worthy, J., Broaddus, K., & Ivey, G. (2001). *Pathways to independence: Reading, writing, and learning in grades 3–8.* New York: Guilford Press.

Index

Note: Page numbers in *italic* type refer to figures or tables.

158 THE LEARNING
COMMUNITIES
GUIDE TO
IMPROVING
READING
INSTRUCTION

**CORWIN
PRESS**

The Corwin Press logo—a raven striding across an open book—represents the union of courage and learning. Corwin Press is committed to improving education for all learners by publishing books and other professional development resources for those serving the field of K–12 education. By providing practical, hands-on materials, Corwin Press continues to carry out the promise of its motto: **"Helping Educators Do Their Work Better."**